The Adoption Option

The Adoption Option

Choosing and Raising the Shelter Dog for You

by Eliza Rubenstein and Shari Kalina

Howell Book House

HOWELL BOOK HOUSE

A Simon & Schuster Macmillan Company
1633 Broadway
New York, NY 10019-6785

MACMILLAN is a registered trademark of Macmillan, Inc.

Library of Congress Cataloging-in-Publication Data

Rubenstein, Eliza

The adoption option : choosing and raising the shelter dog for you/by
Eliza Rubenstein and Shari Kalina.
        p.   cm.
Includes bibliographical references (p.169).
ISBN 0-87605-425-4
1. Dogs.   2. Animal shelters.   I. Kalina, Shari.
II. Title.
SF427.R85   1996
636.7'0887—dc20   95-4725
                                                   CIP

Book design by Amy Peppler Adams–designLab, Seattle

Contents

Foreword

As I write this, my ten pounds of Poodle mix and solid heart, Ziggy, snuggles in my lap, snoring slightly. I reach down to stroke his soft fur and am reminded of the day I adopted him from the shelter I was running. He had been turned in by a family member of his original owner, who had recently moved to a nursing home that would not accept animals. Now, four years later, he is joined in my home by Sandy, a retriever mix; Lilly, a kittenish fluff ball; and Blanche, an older, white, sort-of-Persian cat beginning to show her age these days. They are four members of my family whose presence in my life provides a source of deep joy and satisfaction for my daughter, my wife, and me. They help create and keep secure a place from which I draw something that allows me to keep working in the field of animal protection, as I have done for over sixteen years.

Because I have worked in animal shelters for so long, my pleasure at welcoming a book like *The Adoption Option* is great. Bringing any animal into one's life is a wonderful event; when the animal comes from an animal shelter, the event is particularly special. And although many victims of pet overpopulation don't wind up in shelters—they may be abandoned on the street, left behind in a deserted house, or even dumped in a garbage can—the ones who do make it to a shelter are lucky enough to have a roof over their heads, food and water to nourish them, and a chance at a new beginning. That's where you come in. By adopting from animal shelters, each one of us can help these facilities do the important job they've set out to do: protect and care for homeless animals.

If you have decided to bring a shelter animal into your life, or are considering such a step, this book can help you plan the process and answer the many questions you are bound to have about choosing and caring for a shelter dog (some may also apply to cats!). Just remember that the day-to-day experiences which make up a life with a companion animal—even the difficult ones—are part of the journey. So enjoy your new companion as he or she will undoubtedly enjoy you, and relish the fact that you have made a significant contribution to helping animals—just through your adoption of a single one.

Kenneth White
Vice President, Companion Animals/Field Services
The Humane Society of the United States
March 19, 1995

About the Authors

It's only polite that we introduce ourselves to you before we start giving you suggestions about adopting a dog, and it's only right we spread around some credit to all the people and pups who have had a hand (or paw) in the making of this book. *The Adoption Option* has evolved out of our years of happy and educational experiences with people and dogs, and we hope it will help to create some happy and educational experiences for you and *your* dog, too.

Our love of dogs brought us together in 1991 when we were both students at Oberlin College in Oberlin, Ohio. Shari, a longtime shelter enthusiast and volunteer, had founded Oberlin's student-staffed OASIS Animal Shelter a year earlier at the age of nineteen. Eliza, at seventeen, had been training dogs for six years, working as a shelter volunteer for four and writing a column in *Front and Finish: The Dog Trainer's News* for three. At the time we had one dog apiece; now we're up to five total (Ralph, Ava and Tyler Kalina, and Alfy and Sebastian Rubenstein), four of whom were adopted from the OASIS Shelter and all of whom are the greatest dogs in the world. You'll see each of them at least once in the pages that follow.

We've heard a lot of good questions during our years of working with people and their adopted dogs, and perhaps the most common—and the one that always used to leave us scratching our heads—is "Why isn't there one single book that covers the whole adoption process?" This book is, in a way, our answer. We wish you all the best in your life with your dog(s), and we hope the experience of dog adoption will be as delightful and thrilling for you as it has been for us. Good Luck!

From left to right: Ralph, Shari, Ava, Sebastian, Eliza and Alfy (*Photograph by House of Photography*).

Acknowledgments

A handful of special people deserve a pat on the head for their help and inspiration: thanks to Mordecai Siegal, Sue Jeffries and Len Podis for their writerly advice and encouragement; Jessica Rubenstein, Walter Jo, Kristel Brodsky, Mary Dellorto, Maren Eliason, Chris Dane, Erika Giddings, Jack Glazier, Laurel Kristick, Rachel Levine, Amy Morgan, Kathleen Perry, Laura Ruff, Cheryl Smith, Nancy Steinbrecher and Suzette Wood for the photographs of their adopted dogs that appear throughout the book; Shawn Kessler and the Montgomery County Humane Society for the photo opportunity; Nancy Matlock and the Kennelwood training staff and Vera Opel and the OASIS staff for being great dog people and great influences; Dr. James Cobb and Dr. Gary Schwartz for their veterinary know-how; Rachel Lamb, the Humane Society of the United States and the American Humane Association for their artwork and encouragement; Carol Lea Benjamin for being a pioneer in this worthy field; all the people who offered us their photographs, suggestions and well-wishes; and our families (especially Barbara, Ted and Robin Kalina, and Nancy, Bill and Jessica Rubenstein) and friends for, well, everything.

An extra bit of biscuit for our buddies Alfy, Ava, Ralph, Sebastian and Tyler, as well as CAT the cat and B.J. and C.J. the ferrets, who are great companions despite not being canine . . . and finally, a loving thank you to the big-hearted and sloppy-jowled Barney Kalina, 1989–1992, who inadvertently set all these crazy wheels spinning.

Carmen's Story

Carmen is a good dog.

She loves to cuddle or play with the members of the Brauchler family, but she also knows when it's time to quit. Because she knows how to walk nicely on a leash, she gets to go places with them, but she's also willing to stay home without complaint. When she hears the thrilling words "Carmen, let's go get the kids!" every afternoon, she heads for the door, ready to embark on her daily journey to the bus stop. She graduated at the top of her obedience class. She's gentle, she's well-mannered, and—except for one shredded table leg back when she didn't know any better—she's never destructive. She's crazy about her people, and they're crazy about her.

But if you'd seen Carmen a year ago, you'd have seen a very different dog. A young couple out for a walk on a muddy March morning discovered the three-month-old Sheltie-Beagle-terrier mix and her three sisters curled up and crying in a cardboard box in a field. The couple took pity on the abandoned pups and took them to a nearby animal shelter, where for the first time the four littermates ate real meals, slept on blankets in a clean cage and visited a vet. Shelter volunteers played fetch with them, took them for walks and gave them baths and brushings. It took a while, but Carmen and her sisters learned not to shrink into a corner of their cage when people approached, and they no longer cringed and ducked when someone tried to pet them or pick them up.

Life in the shelter was a definite improvement. After all, the puppies had probably spent their first twelve weeks eating scavenged scraps for dinner, sleeping out in the cold, and running for cover when they spotted a human. They should have been living it up and exploring the joys of puppyhood, but instead they'd been struggling for survival.

Now, finally, they were safe and cared for, but living in a raucous kennel with a dozen other dogs wasn't as cozy as having families of their own, and vying for the attention of a few volunteers wasn't as nice as being someone's number-one dog. The shelter was a good start, but it was hardly a *home*. One by one, Carmen's three sisters left the shelter. One joined a big family with lots of kids; one became the first "baby" of a newlywed couple; the third was taken home by a smitten shelter volunteer. But Carmen stayed—until Marilyn and Bill Brauchler arrived at the shelter one May afternoon and gave her the lucky break she needed. The Brauchlers had done their homework, so they took their time in choosing Carmen, and they knew they'd made a good decision.

Of course, when they took her home, they began to wonder what they'd gotten themselves into. The first night, Carmen lived up to her operatic name by crying all night long. Luckily, her performance was only a one-time phenomenon, but there were other problems to work through, too.

For one thing, Carmen was still terribly shy and submissive. When visitors came to the door, she hid behind it. She was sure that the staircase was a medieval torture device designed just for her. And as for that horrible monster called the vacuum cleaner, well, forget it.

But the Brauchlers didn't get frustrated, and they didn't rush things. They took Carmen for walks all over the neighborhood until she got used to the sights and sounds and smells of the real world. They introduced her slowly to the stairs, the vacuum cleaner, and the other scary stuff lurking around the house. They let her know that they thought she was the greatest pup in the world and that she didn't need to be afraid of them. And they didn't waste any time signing her up for an obedience class.

It took three months or so before Carmen really got over her worries. But these days, Carmen's a contented pup. She's sweet, smart, self-assured, and a loved and valued member of the family. When someone comes to the door, she wags her tail and smiles, but she never jumps. And—this just might be her crowning achievement—she was the only dog in her obedience class who was able to resist the urge to chase a bouncing tennis ball during a group sit-stay exercise. The Brauchlers knew Carmen would have special needs and special problems, but they also knew she could turn into a very special pet.

And she has.

Carmen's story is a good story. But it's not the only story. The terrible truth is that for every shelter dog who finds a happy, stable home,

Brian, Marilyn, Alison, Bill and Carmen (*Photograph by Kaleidoscope Portraits*).

there are dozens who don't. By conservative estimates, four to six million dogs and puppies are killed in American animal shelters and pounds every year—four to six million wonderful animals, young and old, male and female, purebred and mixed-breed, full of personality and potential. Most haven't done anything wrong; they're no less affectionate or intelligent or beautiful than their luckier counterparts. Almost any of them could become someone's ideal companion, but few ever get the chance.

Where do all these dogs come from? Some are the products of unplanned matings between stray dogs, or between pets whose people have neglected to neuter them and have allowed them to roam. Some were bred by people who thought puppy-raising would be fun and profitable, until they discovered how much time, energy, and money the process required, and how difficult it was to find homes for the pups. Some shelter dogs used to be family pets but were discarded when they ate too much, barked too loudly, or took too long to housebreak. Some have moved from home to home and shelter to shelter for years. Many unwanted and abandoned dogs don't even make it to animal shelters: They grow up on the streets, living rewardless lives and dying young.

We humans, unfortunately, have helped to create this problem by failing to live up to our end of the dog-human contract, the contract which says that our dogs will give us their loyalty and respect in return for our care and protection. Loving our dogs isn't enough. We also have a responsibility to shield them from danger, to meet their physical needs and to keep them from producing more puppies and adding to the already staggering number of homeless dogs. And we have a responsibility not to give up on them when things don't work out as perfectly as we'd like. Some of us aren't living up to those responsibilities.

You may not be one of the people causing the problem. But you can be one of the people who helps to fix it. You can give a homeless puppy or dog the love and guidance she needs—and find yourself a terrific, one-of-a-kind friend, too. We're not going to tell you that every adoption is a fairy tale, because that would be a lie. Adopted dogs eat furniture, stain carpets, pull at their leashes and bark at the wrong times just like other dogs—sometimes even more, thanks to their often checkered pasts. An adopted dog is a special dog: she'll require an extra share of your patience and understanding in order to smooth out her rough edges and become a civilized family member, but, chances are, her devotion and appreciation will more than compensate. By turning one dog's difficult past into a promising future, you can not only enrich her life and yours but also play a small yet significant part in solving the larger problem of pet overpopulation.

This book is designed to help *you* help a dog in need. It answers many of the questions we've heard (and a few we haven't heard often enough!) during our years of working at animal shelters and educating dogs and their people. So we hope you'll read it through—along with as many other good dog books as you can find—before you start looking for a pup. It will give you the information—and, we hope, the inspiration—you'll need to adopt the right dog for you, and to make your relationship as successful as Carmen and her family's. We want you to enjoy and appreciate your adopted dog to the fullest.

And you can.

CHAPTER 1

Is Adoption Right for You?

There's just something about dog people," a friend told us once. "The ability to communicate with and love another species seems to make them kinder, more understanding, more fun."

We probably don't need to waste too much space convincing you of the joys of having a dog. You already know how much kindness, understanding, and fun dogs provide for us. You already know (or, at least, can imagine) the delight of having a favorite pup put her warm snuffling snout on your knee, or try to climb into bed with you and hog all the blankets, or bring you a sloppy toy in hopes of a game of fetch. If you're like us, you have to scratch the ears of every friendly dog you meet, and you'd rather see Benji than Geraldo on your TV screen. Dogs have probably put lots of goofy grins on your face, and you're not alone. Dogs bring our lives spontaneity and security at the same time. Their antics remind us not to take ourselves too seriously, and their staunch, even stubborn, adoration always make us wonder what in the world we've done to deserve such devotion.

There's another side to the dog-human relationship, of course: the training, the feeding, the cleaning—the energy and expense of having a dog. Sometimes we refer to it as the less appealing side of the deal, the necessary but unpleasant tradeoff. But perhaps that's not entirely fair; after all, as any true dog lover knows, there's a certain joy in attending to the needs of a favorite pup, and while housebreaking and flea-dipping may not be anyone's preferred pastimes, they're just a couple of the responsibilities we undertake in order to ensure that we earn the affection and trust of the canines we love. The give-and-take nature of the dog-human relationship is what makes caring for a dog more demanding than, say, caring for a fish—and it's also what makes it, for many of us, far more rewarding.

Lots of maudlin stuff has been written about the virtues of the humble dog, about how she'll forgive you for ignoring or hurting her, how she'll idolize you even if you barely pay attention to her, how she lives only to please and serve you even if you don't care about pleasing and serving her. That may have some truth in it, but let's face it: sometimes people propagate that kind of "flattery" in order to make themselves, and all of us humans, feel less guilty about the fact that we don't always give our dogs the fair treatment and loving attention they deserve. It's *not* all right to deprive our dogs of the time, care and love they need, and then console ourselves with the notion that their saintly doggy natures will somehow fill in the gaps we've left. That just makes for miserable dogs—and miserable people, too, because the real truth is that you get just about as much respect and devotion from a dog as you give to her.

Understanding your duties and responsibilities, then, is the first step in deciding to add a dog—especially an adopted dog—to your family. *Any* dog will require a hefty amount of your time, space, supervision, discipline and love; an adopted dog, who hasn't grown up with all the advantages of living with your family, will need extra helpings of each. Consider carefully what you will owe your chosen dog before you choose her; make yourself a list of the pros and cons of adoption and discuss with everyone else in your family what adjustments you'll all need to make.

It's tempting, upon learning of the horrors of pet overpopulation and reading a story as happy as Carmen's, to want to dash to the nearest animal shelter and scoop up armloads of dogs. That's an urge that all big-hearted, dog-adoring people know well. Before you hop in the car, though, take the time to ensure that you and your family are truly ready and willing to adopt a canine companion. None of us can solve the overpopulation problem all alone, but each of us can make the world better for one homeless dog—provided we choose and raise our special dogs wisely and conscientiously.

The decision to introduce a dog into your household should never, never be made hastily; it deserves to be contemplated and discussed thoroughly with everyone involved. Quick, impulsive decisions, after all, account for why a lot of dogs end up in animal shelters in the first place, so weigh *all* the aspects of living with a dog before you determine to pursue the Adoption Option. Take your time. The more patient and careful you are now, the more delightful your years with your canine friend will be!

What All Dogs Need: Things To Consider Before Getting Any Dog

Do you have time for a dog?

Pups are precious; so is time, and you've probably already got dozens of people and obligations making demands on yours, right? A dog—particularly one new to your home—will demand a good deal of your attention as well, and she probably won't adjust her needs precisely to your schedule! So if everyone in your family spends long hard days at work and school, or if you're often out of town or away from home, ask yourself how many free hours you'll have left for a dog. Is your life feeling particularly hectic and crazy and stressful these days? Then you might be better off waiting to get a dog—or getting another companion, perhaps an adopted cat, that will be somewhat more self-sufficient.

Now, that doesn't mean that you have to quit your job or be eternally racked with guilt if you intend to adopt a dog; after all, someone has to pay for the dog food, and your dog (with proper training and socialization) will understand that she can—and must—pass time by herself now and then. Even so, before you adopt a dog, be sure that your schedule and your obligations won't keep you from spending as many happy hours with her as you'll certainly want to. It's really not fair to adopt a dog if you're going to be at work all day long and too exhausted to play with her when you get home. We've watched a lot of tearful people give up their dogs for adoption, having realized too late that they didn't have time for them. It's far better to make that realization now than to risk making yourself and your dog very unhappy later on.

In the beginning, your adopted dog will require lots of guidance as she adjusts to her new lifestyle: you're going to have to show her what life is like in the wild, wild world outside the shelter, and what's expected of her. For starters, most shelter dogs aren't fully housebroken, so you'll need to supervise her especially scrupulously during the first week or more, and you'll have to make yourself available for trips outside as she adapts to your tidy ways (we'll discuss housebreaking in more detail in Chapter 5). If you and your family aren't home during the day, you may need to find a friend or neighbor who can step in as your dog's daytime escort in the beginning in order to keep her on her schedule. Or you can look into the "dog day care" programs that are becoming more widely available at boarding kennels or through pet-sitting services.

Just like kids, dogs need education and etiquette in order to be able to function as responsible citizens—and in order not to drive you crazy. Training makes for happy dogs and happy people, so plan to sign yourself and your new buddy up for obedience lessons (usually a commitment of one to two hours of class time per week), and count on daily training sessions of ten to thirty minutes with your dog, even after basic training is over. Not only will she learn her manners, become more responsive and less troublesome, and earn a snazzy doggie diploma that you can hang on your wall, but you'll both find that learning your exercises together and developing a common vocabulary is a terrific way—perhaps the best possible way—to understand your dog and to form a long-lasting and rewarding bond with her.

Naturally, you'll also want to be around to spend "Quality Canine Time" with your new friend. Throughout her life, she'll need to be fed and walked regularly, and she'll be grateful for every spare second you can spend playing or cuddling with her. Dogs are great antidotes to the stresses of our often superhuman schedules. Just be certain that you'll have time in *your* schedule to enjoy your dog's company.

Do you have room for a dog?

"We really can't keep her," a young couple told us cheerfully as they returned their gangly, energetic, unmannered six-month-old German Shepherd mix to the shelter. "When we adopted her a few months ago, we had no idea she'd grow so big and need so much room."

That's a common refrain at animal shelters. People tend to forget—even if they've been warned, and especially when they're face to face with a sweet and conveniently small puppy—that dogs of all sizes take up plenty of space. They need room to grow, room to run around, room to play with you, room to be by themselves and give you some time apart from them (and vice versa!) now and then. And while dogs are generally pretty genial about squeezing into whatever space they're allotted, it will be unfair and frustrating for both you and your dog if you adopt a pup who really doesn't fit into your home.

Do your living quarters feel cramped already? Then you may not want to decrease your oxygen supply even more. At any rate, you'll have to give careful thought to the size and type of dog you choose. It's a myth that dogs can't

Samantha, a baby Border Collie mix, needs room to stretch her legs—in all directions!

live happily in urban settings, but while there are probably a handful of mammoth Great Dane–Irish Wolfhound crosses or hyperactive retriever mixes living happily in high-rise apartments, common sense indicates that some dogs just aren't designed to fit into such small surroundings. If you long for a big, boisterous dog, make sure you can accommodate her; that probably means several walks a day for life. (Apartment dwellers should remember, too, that even cosmopolitan dogs need walks, which may entail climbing flights of stairs several times a day; the bright side is that you and your dog will develop impressive leg muscles during the housebreaking process!)

If you live in a house, then a fenced yard or pen will serve you and your dog well (in fact, some animal shelters may *require* you to have one before they'll let you adopt a dog). That does *not* mean you can leave your dog outside all the time; there is no such thing as an "outside dog," and there's really no sense in getting a dog if she's not going to be able to live with you. Still, dogs love the chance to stretch their legs and enjoy the outdoors—some more than others—and they should *never* be left to run free, even in secluded and seemingly safe areas. Far too many dogs get lost, stolen or injured in car accidents or fights because their people failed to keep them home. At best, letting a dog run free is irresponsible; at worst, it's terribly dangerous, so don't worry that you'll be cramping your dog's style by setting boundaries for her. (We remember all too well a Gordon Setter who used to show up at the animal shelter regularly after wandering away from home. His owner would leave him there for a day or two and then show up to claim him, thanking us for the free room and board and apparently never hearing us when we urged him to keep closer tabs on his dog. Chances are, that dog has been lost or killed since we last saw him.)

Keep in mind, though, that a four-foot fence won't keep in a determined medium- to large-sized dog, and a fence with openings in it or holes beneath it will do little to deter a smaller canine from performing a Houdini-style escape act. Some neighborhoods don't allow fences; if yours is such a community, you may need to consider installing an underground, electronic "fence" that will teach your dog (after a short training period) to stay within the boundaries of your property. (Electric fences aren't without their drawbacks; for one thing, they do a good job of keeping most dogs *in*, but they do nothing to keep strange dogs and people *out*.)

But whatever your indoor or outdoor accommodations are, remember that they won't replace daily walking and outdoor play, since dogs left to their own devices tend not to be terribly innovative when it comes to entertaining and exercising themselves. Dogs can become couch potatoes just as easily as people can, and even in a big luxurious house with a rolling green yard, your pup may decide to spend her days asleep in a corner or watching talk shows from the easy chair if you don't encourage her to stretch her legs now and again.

Take a look around the inside of your house or apartment, too. Do you have brand-new wall-to-wall carpeting that you don't want pawprinted? Are there a lot of valuable or fragile items in your home that a bored or rowdy dog could chew or break? (You can, of course, teach your dog to respect your furniture and your stuff, and you can designate certain rooms as "off limits"—more on that in Chapters 5 and 6— but it's a rare dog who lives her entire life without a few little errors in judgment.) Close your eyes and picture your living quarters with a dog running around. The image should make you grin, not cringe!

Are you allowed to have a dog?

Too often, renters bring home dogs only to discover that their landlords won't allow them to stay. By all means, if someone else owns the apartment or house you live in, make sure that he or she will permit you to have a dog! (It's important to get his or her consent in writing for later security, too; that will ensure that your landlord won't renege on your agreement later on, and some shelters will require you to present proof of his or her permission before they'll let you adopt a dog.)

If, by the way, your landlord is reluctant to assent at first, don't abandon your canine dreams just yet—you may be able to change his or her mind. Understand that his or her hesitation is probably the result of previous tenants who were not as conscientious as you will be. Landlords lose a lot of time, money, and property because of renters who let their dogs destroy or dirty their apartments or houses. Set up a time to talk calmly with your landlord and convince him or her that you're different. Discuss your understanding of the responsibilities of having a dog; offer to pay a damage deposit; agree to adopt a dog that is over a certain age or under a certain size. In short, determine your landlord's specific concerns (and some landlords, when pressed for precise reasons for their objection to dogs, will come up rather empty) and seek ways to alleviate them or to reach a compromise. Then *put your agreement in writing,* and by all means stick to your part of the deal.

We want to mention, too, the issue of college students who adopt dogs while in school. It's become somewhat of a trendy thing to do, since getting a dog often seems like the perfect way to make campus life complete, especially for students—but it's not always a great idea. Students' tight budgets, small living spaces and hectic schedules usually can't accommodate a dog's needs, and, too frequently, students graduate or go home for the summer and fail to make provisions for their pups. Animal shelters in college towns are filled with abandoned dogs every year after commencement time.

Don't even think of adopting a dog if you live in a dormitory, apartment, or house where pets are forbidden. Either you'll have to hide her so carefully that she'll never have any fun, or she'll be discovered and you'll have to give her up. Don't adopt a dog with the understanding that she is to be a "communal" pet; it's fine for several friends or housemates to contribute to her care, but one person needs to assume primary responsibility for her expenses and education. And don't adopt a dog if you know, or even *suspect,* that you won't be able to keep her after you graduate or move on.

This isn't to say that dogs can never lead the academic life; in fact, both of us had dogs (six total, plus a handful of temporary "foster dogs"!) throughout our college careers. That meant we had to find housing where pets were allowed, stretch our budgets to buy their dog food and supplies, come home between classes to let them out, come home early enough every night to feed them, take them with us or make boarding arrangements for them during vacations and—most importantly—understand that while college would last only a few years, our dogs would be around for many more, and they would come with us wherever we went after graduation.

If you're a student, please think very, very carefully about whether you can make a long-term commitment to a dog. And if you're concerned that you can't, then wait a few years to get your own dog, and spend time with other people's pups or volunteer at a local animal shelter in the meantime!

Can you afford a dog?

Although adopting a shelter dog won't cost as much up front as purchasing a purebred, it's never cheap to raise a dog well. You can keep the cost manageable by shopping intelligently and avoiding unnecessary expenses, but it's smart to whip out your pencil and paper and do a little arithmetic beforehand to determine whether a dog will fit comfortably into your budget.

In the last several years, large discount pet-supply stores have become popular, to the delight of thrifty dog lovers everywhere, and there's probably one near you. Or you can mail-order much of what your dog needs from a wholesale distributor; ask your veterinarian or look in a dog magazine for the addresses of such outlets.

Unless your dog has special nutritional needs, she can live happily and healthily on a regular diet of dry dog food. Check the local prices on high-quality commercial kibble; your dog doesn't necessarily have to eat the fanciest, most expensive gourmet brand, but she also shouldn't eat low-grade, no-name-brand food, which may not meet her needs and can lead to dry skin, dull fur and eyes, low energy, diarrhea and poor overall health. Most dogs don't need canned or semi-moist food, which is more expensive and often less nutritionally complete than dry food, but they'll love having a few spoonfuls of it with their dinner now and then as an hors d'oeuvre.

Count on setting aside some funds for veterinary expenses as well. You'll be responsible for yearly check-ups and vaccinations, of course. In most parts of the country, dogs need to take medicine to prevent heartworm, a potentially fatal parasite transmitted by mosquitoes. Heartworm preventative can be taken as a daily tablet or a once-a-month pill.

The former costs several dollars a month, the latter, slightly more. And most dogs, at some point in their busy lives, will need to be treated for some illness or injury, though you can minimize that risk by keeping your dog vaccinated, well-fed and supervised.

Spaying or neutering—one of the most important things you can do for your dog, as we'll discuss in Chapter 5—may have already been done by the shelter, but otherwise it will probably cost between $50 and $150 if it's done by a vet in private practice. Many shelters and humane societies, though, offer low-cost spay-and-neuter programs that can reduce that cost substantially. And at many shelters, part of your adoption fee will be applied to the price of the operation.

Obedience-school tuition is another investment that will pay huge dividends to you and your dog. Training classes, which generally last for eight to ten weeks, usually cost between $30 and $125—more if your instructor is well-known or if you opt for private lessons.

Crates, leashes, collars, brushes, shampoo and other supplies will set you back a few bucks as well, but with a little smart shopping and creative recycling, you can keep yourself from going bankrupt over your dog's hardware. Chapter 5 will provide a more complete list of what trappings your new dog will need and how you can outfit her with hand-me-downs if you don't care to spend your savings on fancy beds and doggie dinnerware!

If you're a traveling type, you'll need to find either a good, licensed boarding kennel or a pet-sitter in your area for those times when you can't take your pup on the road with you. Boarding a dog generally costs between $10 and $15 a day; pet-sitting (in which someone will come to your house to tend to your pup's needs) may run a bit higher.

And, of course, you'll surely want to shower your new buddy with treats and toys and presents. That's fine as long as you don't overdo it. After all, if you lavish *too* many spoils upon your dog, she may become ill-adjusted and need a canine psychologist—and we hear that they charge up to $200 an hour.

Do you have children or elderly family members to consider?
If you live alone, you can skip this part. But if not, remember that *all* the members of your family will have to live with a new dog, and all of them need to be prepared and willing to adapt to her presence. It'll be an adjustment and a commitment for everybody, and especially for any young or old people in your household.

Mira and adopted spaniel mix Tela make a great pair because they've both learned how to play by the rules and respect each other.

If you've just introduced a new baby to the family, or if you're planning to do so in the next couple of years, congratulations are in order, but a new dog may not be. After all, it takes even more time and energy to raise a kid than it does to raise a dog, and trying to do both at once can make even the coolest, calmest family resemble something out of a bad sitcom. Some people adopt puppies in hopes that their puppies and their babies will grow up together as best friends. Sadly, the work of rearing *two* little darlings often becomes overwhelming, and the pups too frequently end up neglected or returned to the shelter. So if you have a two-legged baby, it makes more sense to wait until he or she is a little older to add a four-legged one to the family.

Is it true that kids and dogs "go together"? Sure it is, although most child-and-canine partnerships aren't quite as idyllic as Timmy and Lassie's—at least at first. Children of any age will need to be taught how to play with and respect a dog (more on this follows in Chapter 5), and your dog will need to learn how to play nicely with them, too. Your children should understand their responsibilities *before* a dog enters the picture. Let them spend time around other people's dogs under your supervision. Talk to them intelligently about what they'll be expected to do for the new dog and how they'll have to treat her. Make sure they know that she'll be a friend and family member, not a stuffed animal, and that they can't tuck her into a closet if they lose interest in her or become too busy to pay attention to her.

Please *don't* get a dog with the understanding that your child or children will be entirely responsible for her care. Kids certainly can and should participate in the duties and the fun, but raising and training a dog is an adult job. Kids often find that it's more work than they can handle, and parents usually end up picking up the slack sooner or later. Too many families adopt dogs so that the kids will "learn responsibility," but that's backwards: Children need to prove their responsibility *before* a dog ever enters the picture. Older children and teenagers may be prepared for the duties of dog care if they are particularly mature and responsible, but be sure they've demonstrated their commitment and their understanding of what dog care entails before you start looking for a dog, and be sure to make provisions for when the kids go off to college or move out of the house.

Beware of pet allergies, which are especially common in children. It's simple to test for allergies before you get a dog, and in many cases it's easy to treat them. It's heartbreaking, though, to have to give up a dog because you discovered too late that she made someone in the family sneeze or wheeze. (You can reduce the problem by choosing a dog with an allergy-friendly coat—more on that in Chapter 2—and by keeping her well-brushed and the house vacuumed.)

Older or infirm relatives, or family members with physical limitations, may not appreciate the acquisition of a large, noisy or boisterous canine, though they may greatly enjoy the company of a smaller or more laid-back canine friend. It's been proven over and over that pets are beneficial to emotional and physical health, so a dog may be just what the doctor ordered, but if you're doing a lot of caregiving for a relative, make sure you'll have the time and willingness to add a dog to your charges.

In any case, be sure to discuss thoroughly the responsibilities of dog ownership with everyone who will be living—or spending a lot of time—in your household. No need to turn your home into the next Animal House due to lack of planning!

Do you have other pets to consider?

Four-footed family members have to get used to having a new dog on the premises, too. Dogs usually like the company; they're pack animals, after all, and they enjoy playing and exercising and napping with each other. (People often find that it's actually easier in some ways to care for two dogs than to have just one, since pooches in pairs tend to entertain each other.) But dogs aren't any more immune to that green-eyed monster called jealousy than we humans are. If you have, for example, an older dog who is used to being showered with *all* your attention and affection, he or she may find it tough to share you with another pup. If your dog tends to be especially protective of you or aggressive toward other dogs, you may be in for a lot of refereeing if you introduce a new one to the household. Except in cases of serious aggression, you can

The black spot in this picture is eight-week-old Sebastian, whom eight-year-old Alfy graciously welcomed into the fold.

usually prevent or ease the power struggles that sometimes arise in multi-dog homes, but it can be exhausting to serve as mediator, especially in the beginning.

What about cats? Well, canine–feline relations aren't really as hopelessly deadlocked as most Saturday-morning cartoons make them seem. We know lots of families in which cats and dogs live together either as good friends or, at least, as peaceful cohabitants. Cats are masters of avoidance and escape, and most dogs learn to leave them alone fairly quickly. So unless you have a particularly nervous cat or adopt a particularly unrelenting dog, you can almost certainly keep them from becoming the next Snoopy and the cat next door.

Can you give a dog the love and attention she needs throughout her life?

This criterion is the most difficult of all to quantify, and it's also the most important. We live in a buy-it-now-and-throw-it-away-later society, full of disposable this and disposable that, and it's terribly disturbing to realize that so many of us have begun to think of living beings in those terms. If this chapter has sounded in any way over-cautious or discouraging, it's only because too many people adopt dogs for the wrong reasons: because they thought their kids might enjoy a pet, because they wanted a guard dog to protect the house, because they saw a particular pooch and thought it was cute, because it seemed like the right thing to do at the time. Then, when dog-rearing becomes a little too much trouble or when life gets a little too hectic for comfort, they toss their dogs away like trash. It's sad, it's unfair, and it's distressingly common.

A good adoption will leave you both smiling.

Adopting a dog means making a promise. When you sign a contract at an animal shelter, you vow not just to pay her adoption fee or get her spayed or vaccinated, but also to be her friend and guardian for as long as she's around. That means taking her outside even when it's sleeting, taking her to obedience class even when your feet hurt after a lousy day at work, and giving her tummy rubs even when you're mad at her for chewing up your favorite tube socks. It means making arrangements for her when you can't be around to look after her, and taking her with you if you move. It means treating her with respect, teaching her how to live among humans and sometimes just letting her be a wild and crazy dog.

That's a lot to promise. Of course, you'll get a lot in return, too: a wagging tail to meet you at the door when you come home, a tireless tennis-ball-fetching partner, a conglomeration of charming canine quirks for you to discover and enjoy. It's a fabulous deal as long as you're able to uphold your part of it. So before you start looking for a dog, examine very closely your reasons for wanting one.

- Are you looking for a friend who will depend on you for all her needs for perhaps the next fifteen years?

- Are you ready to give a dog all the care and love she needs, and to put aside your own needs now and then for her sake?

- Are you thinking as much of her happiness and need for companionship as of your own?

If you can answer "yes" to these questions, then you're well on your way to being a fantastic friend to a special adopted dog.

Special Dogs, Special Needs

Dogs are dogs, and that's the first thing to keep in mind as you go about the process of adopting a pet. A dog from a shelter isn't really so different from her blueblooded counterparts: she has the same basic physical and emotional needs and the same capacity to learn and love. But she's special, too, in ways you'll want to be aware of.

For one thing, she's very likely a unique combination of breeds. Though some shelter dogs (more and more every year, in fact) are purebred, the majority are mixed-breeds. Some are easy to identify as crosses of particular breeds; others defy all attempts at genealogy. One disadvantage to adopting a mixed-breed dog is the uncertainty it involves. If you adopt a puppy of unknown breeding, for example, you may not know whether she will grow up to be tiny or huge, active or lethargic, outgoing or reserved, hooked on herding or fond of fetching—characteristics you might be better able to predict with a purebred, although Chapter 2 will help you recognize potential physical and temperamental traits in the mixed-breed shelter dogs you visit. If your sights are firmly set on a particular breed, and you can't locate the breed you want at a shelter or through a breed rescue society (see Chapter 2 and Appendix A), you may have to purchase a purebred pup in order to get exactly what you want. With so many wonderful dogs awaiting homes, though, you'll surely be able to find one with most of the traits you are seeking.

You probably won't mind giving your adopted dog the extra doses of love she needs.

When you adopt a shelter dog, you also don't have the benefit of meeting her parents and knowing her family history. You won't know, for instance, whether her mother had health problems that she could have inherited. And you won't know whether her father was extraordinarily hyper or high-strung. (A neat phenomenon called *hybrid vigor,* however, which is also covered in Chapter 2, often works in your favor to produce healthy shelter dogs.) So you'll have to be especially observant and savvy when you choose your shelter pup; Chapter 3 will help you select a winner.

Heredity aside, keep in mind that your adopted dog may have some leftover physical or emotional scars that you'll have to help her forget, even though her basic constitution will be, for the most part, strong and steady if you choose her intelligently. Like Carmen, many shelter dogs have had difficult beginnings and unpleasant pasts. Some have been abused; some have been neglected; all have been abandoned. They may not be ready immediately to trust people—and who can blame them? Fortunately, dogs are extraordinarily forgiving creatures, and they'll almost always respond, sooner or later, to affectionate overtures. Keep in mind, then, that your adopted dog will need extra doses of love, understanding and patience as she learns to place her confidence in you.

The number-one reason dogs are brought to shelters is that they have "behavior problems." That label covers a multitude of common canine sins (non-shelter dogs commit them, too): house-soiling, chewing, digging, general rowdiness or hyperactivity. If one of those bad habits is what landed *your* dog in a shelter, you'll have to be willing to work to overcome it when you bring her home. Chapter 6—and a good obedience class—will help you teach her the ways of her new world.

Remember, too, that your dog will probably have been calling a shelter home for some time, and the rules of the shelter may not quite correspond to the rules of your household. Your dog will have been living in a cage where housebreaking was irrelevant and barking was *de rigueur.* She won't have seen furniture or stairs recently (or perhaps ever), and she won't immediately understand that she isn't allowed to teethe on your couch and climb on your kitchen counters. If she's been living by her own devices for several months or more, she'll need some extra training so that she learns her manners and can live peacefully in your home.

If she's a young puppy—especially if she was taken from her mother and littermates too early—she'll need a lot of socialization from you and your family so that she grows up to be a normal, well-adjusted dog. You'll have to teach her the things she should have learned, but may not have, during her first few weeks of life: how to play, how to respect authority, how to accept correction and praise.

It's *never* too early or late for a dog to learn all these things. While it may take somewhat longer to train and socialize a shelter dog or puppy, you'll find that the training process will bring the two of you even closer together and help you learn to appreciate and respect each other right from the start of your relationship.

One thing your adopted dog *won't* need, by the way, is your pity! We see a lot of adopted dogs who get away with shameful behavior because their people feel sorry for them. And we know many humans who use their dogs' uncertain histories as excuses for all their problems. Your dog needs your understanding and leadership, not your indulgence. That's a fine line: if your dog grew up on the streets, that may explain why she has no qualms about shredding your curtains, but it doesn't give her license to do so. If she was (or may have been) unkindly treated by someone in her past, that may explain why she initially mistrusts people, but it doesn't give her the right to growl or snap at them. It's going to take a magical mixture of forbearance and toughness on your part to help her adjust to the world outside the shelter.

There are many advantages to adopting a shelter dog, too, besides the obvious benefit of helping to ease the dog overpopulation crisis. If you choose carefully, chances are she'll be resilient and cheerful. She'll be a survivor, full of life and ready to make the most of her new situation.

We've heard a lot of shelter-dog adopters say, "I think my dog *knows* I saved her life . . . I think she really appreciates me." Well, we don't have any scientific proof that that's true, but we tend to believe it. (We know of one Samoyed who, only weeks after his adoption, "thanked" his new owner for all his love and careful training by foiling a burglary of his home one night!) Now, we don't promise that your adopted dog will be eternally angelic out of gratitude to you, but we do think dogs know when they've got it good—and shelter dogs, when raised and educated well, have good reason to feel that way. And *you'll* know, every time your dog casts her big loving eyes upon you, that you are responsible for saving her life and making it worth living.

We don't pretend that adopting a shelter dog is going to be all sweetness and light right from the start; that would be dishonest. If you don't prepare yourself for some adjustments and some stress, then you'll very likely find yourself disappointed during your first few weeks of life with your new friend. But you can also prepare yourself for tons of learning, entertainment and fun.

Yes, it's going to take lots of love and work to make any dog, and especially an adopted dog, part of your life. But you'll discover that if you're patient and fair, your dog will meet you halfway. And the two of you will have a wonderful time together.

SUCCESS STORY #1

Doug Duke and Addison
Washington, D.C.

Few gave "Freeway" much of a chance, and in the beginning it did seem that his chances for adjusting to a new home were dim. His temporary name hardly seemed to fit the black, twenty-pound terrier mix with a stocky frame and a tail that curlicued over his back. The rescue league said he'd been named for the place where he was found: a compassionate woman driving to work in rural Maryland saw the still body of a small dog lying on the shoulder of the road. On her way home later, disgusted that the little black dog's body was still there after eight or nine hours, she stopped and was horrified to find him still alive, in shock and terrified of being touched. One of his back legs was broken; most likely, he had been thrown out of a moving car.

Later, at the shelter, despite medical care, food and the soothing voices of the shelter workers, Freeway still wouldn't allow anyone to touch him, and he snarled and snapped if they tried to get within several feet of him. The staff continued to feed him and clean his cage, but two months passed before he finally let a caregiver rub his head and chest.

But his biting—or nipping, really—did not stop, and he was especially unwilling to let men handle him. It seemed likely that he had been subjected to physical abuse before ending up on the road, and he severely mistrusted all people. But the woman running the shelter couldn't bear to give up on him ("his eyes were just so sweet, and he'd been through so much"), and she held out hope for finding him a home where he could continue to recover.

Freeway was in his fourth month at the shelter by the time I came for a visit, and until then, he had not let a male touch him. I was looking for a small dog to share my apartment and office, but I knew it would be hard to open my heart again just eighteen months after my childhood companion, a Peke-a-Poo, had died naturally in his fourteenth year.

To avoid being intimidating, I sat on the floor and let Freeway approach me on his own, and strangely, he was more at ease with me than with my female friend who had come along. He met our stares with the gentlest expression in his eyes and sat very still, preferring to lick our hands rather than be patted on the head. We walked with him and tried to play with him, and after a while he even let me pick him up. He began to follow me around, and as my friend said, he seemed to "choose" me.

"Addison" (a new name for his new life) and I have now been best buddies for nine months, and though he's still wary of strangers, he's completely stopped nipping. We're already close and have a good understanding of each other. I knew how much effort and tolerance he would need, but his progress has exceeded my expectations from the start.

For almost our whole first month together, Addison wouldn't take his eyes off me. If I was in the shower, he waited behind the curtain (probably wondering why I wanted to get so wet), and when I was taking care of bills or talking on the phone, he watched me as if to compile clues about what made this crazy guy tick.

From the beginning, too, he constantly displayed his incredible loyalty. It may sound like a cliché, but rescued animals genuinely seem to show their gratitude to their rescuers. After each meal, Addison comes to me so that I can ask him about his dinner; every time I leave my office, he sits quietly at the mesh screen in the door to await my return; during a kickball game at an outdoor office function, he had my co-workers in hysterics as he ran behind me as fast as he could while I sprinted around the bases.

Addison is a very gentle and quiet little guy, always happy to be included on trips, walks and other outings. He loves to play with my friends, bark at bikes and skateboards, snack on apple slices, sleep on the bed (though he has his very own chair as well) and take afternoon naps on my lap while I'm typing.

I think there's a lot for me to learn from Addison's humble approach to simple pleasures. I find it hard to comprehend how anyone could have ever inflicted any sort of harm on him—or on any other dog, for that matter. Now, however, I'm making sure that he has peace and comfort, can rely on meals and walks and, most of all, experiences a much better side of human beings.

CHAPTER 2

What Kind of Adopted Dog Is Right for You?

S o you've decided that adoption is the way you want to go. Congratulations! You've already made one smart choice, and now it's time to think about making another.

There are two ways to pick a shelter dog. Method #1, which we might call the "Love at First Sight" method, is to go to a local shelter on some sunny morning, walk past the pens and cages until one special pup catches your eyes with hers, bring her home with you and resolve to love her and take care of her forever.

Method #2, the more pragmatic of the two, is to sit down and decide what kind of puppy or dog will best suit your needs and desires; visit shelters, looking until you locate that particular kind of pet; and *then* bring her home and resolve to love her and take care of her forever.

Method #1, though certainly the sentimental favorite, has some serious shortcomings. It generally works pretty well in the movies (doesn't everything?), but real life doesn't always result in such perfect person-dog matches. It's awfully easy to fall in love with a dog immediately, and it's excruciatingly difficult to fall *out* of love with her if you discover that she's unhealthy, for example, or that she's going to be too big for your home or require more grooming than you have time to give her. You may be tempted to take her home against your better judgment, and that could mean problems later on in your relationship. We've seen lots of dogs returned to shelters after the fleeting *je ne sais quoi* that got them adopted wore off!

Another crisis may arise if you go to a shelter intending to fall for one dog and end up falling for all of them. We all know the feeling of "wanting to take them all home." It's a tough urge to resist, and you

You can see why the perilous "Love at First Sight" method is so popular among people who haven't made a "puppy profile" before they visit a shelter.

don't want to go home feeling guilty for being able to take only one. Better to go to the shelter with clear intentions than to find yourself in confused turmoil as you stand amid the cages. So for the sake of both you and your dog, we recommend that you bypass Method #1 and pursue the less dramatic but overall more successful Method #2.

If you have an idea of your desired dog in your mind before you start shelter-shopping, you'll be better able to resist the temptation to adopt a dog who might not be right for your lifestyle. You're more likely to end up with a pup you can live with and one who can live comfortably in your household and within your schedule. This all may seem like a rather cold and businesslike way to make a very warm and personal decision, but if you let your intelligence and discrimination guide you now, you'll find that your emotions are much better served later! Take some time, then, to sit down—along with any other members of your family—and put into writing, with the help of this chapter, a list of the qualities and characteristics you're going to look for in a dog.

As you formulate this master plan, keep in mind that your aim is not to create some fictional, two-dimensional Ideal Dog. There is not one perfect canine for you; there are many who will suit and delight you, and there are none who won't occasionally depart a bit from your dreams. These will serve as guidelines for you to follow, not a prescription that you must meet exactly. You may not get all the traits you want in one dog. After all, what are the odds of finding, say, a six-month-old, male, lap-sized Mastiff mix with fluffy black fur at your local shelter? Even if you could, she'd be full of surprises all her own that you couldn't possibly have imagined! So don't get *too* attached to the dog you're about to put on paper, but do make some decisions about your preferences and resolve to abide by them as well as you can.

Don't assume, either, that just because you pick a dog who seems to fulfill all your dreams, her life with you will be utter perfection from the get-go! Your "profile" will help you find a great dog to start with, but no matter what kind of dog you adopt, she's going to need plenty of socialization and education to help her fit comfortably into your home.

All right, then, what kind of dog *do* you want? As in all stages of the Adoption Option, there's much to consider!

How Old Should Your Dog Be?

Young or "Teenaged" Puppies

In days past there was a lot of prejudice in favor of puppies. Practically any dog book you encountered would have advised you strongly against getting a dog any more than eight weeks old. Listen to this bit of invective from one 1947 manual's section about the evils of grown, pre-owned dogs:

> They may pretend to like you but secretly they are always comparing you unfavorably with their former master . . . Don't buy a grown dog. He will only make your life miserable bragging about his former grandeur.

We rather enjoy this bit of wisdom for its comic value (and we particularly like the James Thurber cartoon that accompanies it, of a big dog glaring judgmentally at his innocent-looking owner), but we have to disagree emphatically with its premise!

Don't misunderstand: puppies are fabulous. They're loving, they're fun to raise and train and they're devastatingly cute. A young pup may be exactly what you want, but there are other options too.

The greatest advantage of adopting a small puppy (from six to twelve weeks old) is that she'll be able to grow up with you; she'll be *your* dog

Mature dogs like Springer Spaniel Buddy can overcome their troubled pasts to become great . . . buddies!

from the start, since the early weeks of a dog's life are when it's easiest for her to bond quickly with a human. You'll get to teach her your ways and your rules before she has a chance to develop too many bad habits of her own (though you can be sure that she'll have managed to invent a few!). You can begin training her nice and early, and sign her up for puppy obedience classes to help her grow into a well-adjusted and well-behaved dog.

Puppy-raising, however, also comes with its share of extra work and occasional irritation. Housebreaking a very young dog is a slow and not particularly thrilling process. She'll probably keep you up nights for a little while. She'll probably go through one or more phases of chewing as she teethes. And she'll need several rounds of vaccinations and veterinary care during her early weeks.

Don't get a young puppy if you're going to have to leave her alone all day. An older dog can spend eight hours by herself without too much trouble, but a pup needs people around to attend to her needs, especially for housebreaking purposes. (Some shelters will not adopt a puppy under twelve or sixteen weeks old to a household in which she'll have to stay alone for more than four hours at a stretch.)

But you'll have the fun of watching her do all the adorable things puppies do—from trying to tote around tennis balls that won't fit in her mouth to tripping over her unwieldy puppy paws to falling asleep on your feet. There's seldom any shortage of cuteness when there's a puppy in the house.

Suppose you like the idea of a young dog but aren't sure you want a tiny puppy. How about a slightly older pup? Shelters are full of three- to nine-month-old dogs, adolescents who have plenty of youthful energy left in them. In general, the older the puppy, the more quickly you'll be able to housebreak her, and the less chewing and fussing you'll have to endure. (By the way, we don't suggest that you get a puppy under six weeks old. At that age, she'll need you to be her "mother," and unless you've had lots of experience raising canine infants, that's more of a challenge than you want to take on.)

Adult Dogs
If you decide a puppy is what you want, you'll probably have no trouble finding one you love in an animal shelter. But most shelter dogs fall into the category of "adult dogs," those over a year old. And although just about all these grown dogs can turn into terrific pets, people sometimes tend to overlook them, thanks in part to myths like the one previously mentioned.

It's true that older shelter dogs, unlike puppies, have probably had pasts which have strongly influenced their personalities. Some have been neglected or abused in their previous homes. Some have never even lived with people. At the opposite end of the spectrum, some have enjoyed happy homes whose dissolutions may have left them confused and depressed. When you adopt an older dog, you're adopting her previous experiences, too, and she'll require your understanding and perseverance as she adjusts to her new life.

But it's *not* true that dogs deliberately dwell on their pasts and hold grudges against their new owners. In fact, they're probably better at "getting on with their lives" than most humans are! We've heard a lot of romantic stories about "one-person dogs"—dogs whose staunch loyalty permits them to love only one person as long as they live—but, to be quite honest, we've never actually met one. Dogs have more than enough love to go around. Your adopted dog, especially if you're conscientious and careful in your selection, will be more than happy to give you her trust—or, at least, the chance to earn it. She'll adore you just as much as if you'd been her one and only person from the beginning— maybe more—and you'll adore her just as much as if she'd always been your dog.

Of course, some of her "past experiences" may work strongly in your favor. Lots of adult shelter dogs are fully or mostly housebroken already. They've probably outgrown some of their puppyish tendencies to chew or to whine during the night. If they've lived in decent homes before, they may even have had some basic training in canine etiquette. Grown dogs are often a good choice if you have children in the house: even though the pairing of puppy and child is about as all-American as that of peanut butter and jelly, puppies are fragile and children can be rough (and as puppies grow into adolescence, they often become too big and rambunctious for kids), so an older dog who has had experience with small people can be an ideal choice for a family.

One more advantage to adopting a full-grown dog is the predictability factor: It's often tough or impossible to know what a shelter puppy will look like when she's all grown up, but with an adult, what you see is pretty much what you get in terms of size and appearance. And that can give you and your dog some real security; after all, more than a few dogs have been (unfairly) returned to shelters because they grew up to be much bigger or furrier than their adopters expected or wanted.

Most dogs in animal shelters aren't more than a few years old, but you'll find some who qualify as canine senior citizens. Sadly, they're the least likely of all the shelter residents to be adopted. But lots of older dogs still have plenty of puppyish energy left in them and make wonderful mature companions—and, especially if they're small, they can have many years left in them. Others may *not* have as much vigor as they did in their youth, and that can make them perfect matches for older or less active people. We've seen a nine-year-old Cocker Spaniel mix become the best buddy of a lonely widower, and a gentle seven-year-old Beagle mix brighten the lives of a young family with children who were afraid of rowdier dogs. So if you don't mind knowing that you may not have quite as many years with your dog as you would with a pup, you might love the company of a pooch with a little grey on her muzzle.

Should You Get a Male or a Female?

Really, this one's your call. Much has been written about the differences between the personalities and temperaments of male and female dogs: it's said, for example, that females are more retiring and docile while males are more dominant and assertive. We suspect, though, that those beliefs are at least as firmly grounded in society's traditional expectations of males and females as they are in reality! Male dogs were once considered the far more desirable and valuable sex, and females wagged along in their shadow. (Says one venerable 1928 volume with kindly condescension, "There is no particular reason why the female should be frowned upon as she is. She cannot help being of the nature she is.") But times are changing. Frankly, we haven't found either sex to be any more intelligent, trainable or friendly than the other. And we've known and trained enough headstrong females and submissive males that we can state confidently that the old generalizations, like most stereotypes, simply aren't accurate enough to be useful.

It *is* true that males tend to be more territorial than females; they mark and defend their property, though neutering helps to alleviate that urge—or, in some dogs, even prevent it if the operation is done early. (Males may also be slightly more apt to roam away from home, but that doesn't mean that females won't take off if left unattended.) If you already have a male dog in the household—especially an unneutered male—and you adopt another male, you may be in for some major spats over who's the top dog. Of course, if you have an unneutered male and you adopt a *female,* you'll need to get her spayed immediately to prevent any trysts from occurring (and you'll probably want to have *him* neutered, too).

Spaying will also keep a female from going into estrus twice a year; that will spare you a good deal of trouble, and it will spare *her,* from being harassed by interested males while she's in heat.

So unless you already have a gender preference, don't worry yourself too much about it. Dogs' personalities have more to do with their individual characters than with their sex.

Big dogs like Rosie, UD, a rescued Doberman, need plenty of room to romp.

How Big Do You Want Your Dog to Be?

Some people are Big Dog People; some people are Little Dog People. Just be certain that the doggie size you have in mind will fit into your home and your life. Pooches the size of ponies won't thrive in small surroundings unless they get lots and lots of exercise to keep from getting bored and out of shape. Tiny toy dogs can get a nice workout by scurrying around the living room, but they run the risk of getting stepped on in households full of busy people, especially children. If you're not sure just how much dog you want in your life, you might want to look for something in the middle.

Big dogs cost somewhat more to maintain, mostly because they eat more than their slighter counterparts; their large-size collars and bowls and crates will also bear a slightly higher price tag. And small dogs can go more places with you: they can travel with you in the cabins of most airplanes, for example, and they're easy to pick up and carry. On the other hand, big dogs can be terrific at retrieving your newspapers and keeping up with you on jogs, and many people like the feeling of security that walking with a large dog can provide.

Bear in mind that medium-sized to large dogs are always easier to find in shelters than small dogs. Lap-sized dogs less frequently find their ways to shelters, and when they do, they're generally snatched up pretty quickly.

A word of caution: if you choose a young puppy, be prepared to be flexible with your weight and height requirements! Tiny puppies have been known to grow up into big dogs, and vice versa. In fact, we've seen both scenarios in our own doggie families: one of us has an eighty-pound terrier mix who was supposed to be small, and the other has a forty-pound Labrador–German Shepherd mix who was supposed to be big. Needless to say, we've forgiven them for not turning out quite as we'd expected!

What Kind of Fur Do You Want Your Dog to Have?

It may sound a little silly, but your dog's coat type is going to be important when it's time for grooming. Just as some of us like to fuss with our hairdos and some of us can't stand to do much beyond wash-and-wear, we all have preferences when it comes to how much time we want to spend on our dogs' appearances. If you know you won't have time to give your dog more than a few minutes of brushing every day and an occasional bath, don't fall in love with a pup with long, silky fur. And if you hate the thought of dog fur on your furniture and floors, don't make any promises to a dog with fluff who's likely to shed a lot.

Kyle's thick fur means lots of brushing for Erika.

Any dog will need regular brushing and bathing in order to keep her coat clean, pretty and healthy. But some doggie tresses require a lot more work (either by you or by a professional groomer) than others. Long or bushy fur gets hopelessly tangled and matted if it isn't combed daily or trimmed. Wiry hair (like a terrier's) needs clipping to keep it neat. Dogs with "double coats" (like Collies and Huskies, who have woolly undercoats and a layer of rougher fur on top) will get weighed down with extra shed fur if they're not kept combed. (Hot summer weather is especially rough on heavy-coated dogs if they're not kept brushed or clipped.) Ungroomed coats aren't just unattractive; they're hot and uncomfortable, and they're perfect hiding places for parasites and infections. We have seen few sights more upsetting than that of Patrick, a Miniature Poodle who arrived at the shelter with his fur so overgrown and matted that he couldn't open his eyes. His knotted fur was full of dirt and bugs; his skin was patchy and covered with sores. It had taken only about a month for him to become such a mess, but it took hours of washing and clipping before he even resembled a Poodle again, and weeks before he began to recover from his neglect.

Some fur is more allergy-friendly than others, too. Dogs with Poodle- or terrier-type coats generally won't shed as much as fluffier pups, so they'll be less likely to irritate sensitive sinuses. Of course, woolly fur (the canine equivalent of "big hair") has its advantages too: Nothing feels better than a soft, plushy dog lying on your feet in December!

What Kind of Personality Do You Want Your Dog to Have?

Many, many people say to us in amazement, "Dogs really do have distinct personalities, don't they?" Anyone who's spent much time in the company of canines knows that there's nothing shocking about that! Just among our own dogs, the variation is tremendous: There's Tyler, who likes teddy bears and snuggling; Ralph, who can stare at one spot for hours and fall asleep sitting up; Ava, who likes to trick her brothers into doing things they shouldn't; Alfy, who likes to be cold, wet, and dirty and has to be in constant physical contact with humans; and Sebastian, who prefers to bury his nose in the corner of the sofa and sing along to Bach on the stereo.

Your dog will have her own unique collection of characteristics, habits, talents, likes and dislikes; and you'll probably keep discovering new ones throughout her life. But make some choices now about what traits you're going to look for when you start seeking the right dog for you.

Like people, dogs have different attitudes toward exercise and activity. Do you want a dog who will be eternally fired up to go running or swimming with you? Or do you prefer one who will be content to curl up on the couch with you while you read a book? If it's important to you to have a dog whose activity level is similar to yours, you'll want to keep that in mind as you visit shelters.

Some people like a dog with *machismo*, while others prefer a more passive pooch. We don't recommend that you choose a puppy or dog who's either very dominant or very submissive, but within the middle ground there's plenty of variation. Assertive dogs may be more difficult to train; they'll probably challenge your authority from time to time, and they'll need solid corrections and strong leadership from you. Meeker dogs won't be as likely to "test" you, but they'll also have to be socialized and trained with extra care, since they may become upset if you correct them too firmly. Chapter 4 will discuss in much more detail how to determine the dominance or submissiveness of the dogs and puppies you'll meet at shelters.

A trait closely related to dominance is protectiveness: do you want a dog who will guard your home vigilantly, or one who will just give you a

Dogs, like people, have different attitudes toward exercise and activity.

warning bark when an unfamiliar person or animal is nearby? It's not fair to expect any dog to be a foolproof alarm system (and it's certainly not all right to get a dog for that sole purpose), but some dogs are naturally watchful and defensive of their territory, while others don't particularly take to sentry duty. Some tend to trust strangers immediately; others are more reserved and less free with their affection. Which type you prefer depends on your lifestyle and what kind of contact your dog will have with other people. (Obviously, you don't want a dog who's so suspicious of people that she either lives in fear or causes you and everyone around you to live in fear.)

Do you like a dog who hangs on you and needs your attention all day long, or are you more partial to an independent pup? Maybe you're flattered by dogs who follow you around the house and want to be petted and loved all the time, or maybe you're just annoyed by them! A dog who is affectionate to the point of obsequiousness may take more readily to training because she'll want to please you and earn your praise. But an independent dog, though perhaps more stubborn, will also be less likely to invade your personal space and make excessive demands on your time.

There are lots of other doggie qualities that fall under the "personality" category, and none of them is easily quantifiable. You probably have canine characteristics in mind that we haven't even mentioned. Why not just brainstorm for a few minutes and come up with a list of adjectives you'd like to be able to apply to your new dog? (You might even rank them in order of importance to you, since, as we've said, you probably won't get every adjective you want in a single dog!) Should she be serious or happy-go-lucky? Soft-spoken or talkative? Quick-witted or simple-minded? Mischievous or predictable? Passionate or blasé?

What Breed or Mix of Breeds Is Right for You?

So, are you feeling a little like Dr. Frankenstein, putting together bits and pieces to create the imaginary dog of your dreams? Well, now that you've given some thought to what qualities you want in your new puppy or dog, you can start to decide what type of dog is most likely to encompass all those chacteristics.

Should you get a mixed breed or a purebred? You can find either in most shelters: by most estimates, up to 25 percent of shelter dogs today are purebreds. The distinction may be important to you, or it may not. What matters most, really, is finding a dog who meets your needs and desires—a dog who *fits*. Perhaps that dog will turn out to be of mixed heritage, or perhaps she'll be a blueblood. You can be sure that her ancestry isn't going to be a prime concern to *her*, but there are some factors that *you* may want to consider.

Mixed breeds used to be labeled unapologetically as second-class citizens. "A purebred dog always looks better than a mongrel," advises one old dog book. "As a class [mongrels] can never hope to equal the true, pure-blooded animals with their generations of unmixed blood," sniffs another.

That kind of "breedism," thank goodness, is falling more and more out of favor as time marches forward! (Credit *Lady and the Tramp* with getting the ball rolling.) "Mixing of blood" doesn't seem quite the crime it once did, and anyone who's ever had a mixed-breed dog will tell you that mutts aren't a bit less beautiful than their purebred counterparts. We've both had purebreds, and we've both had mixes—and they've all been equally wonderful companions, genealogy notwithstanding!

With purebreds, predictability enters the picture again: when you adopt a dog of a particular breed, you know approximately what she'll look like, and to some extent you know what kind of personality she'll have. Of course, there's much variation within every breed—not all Golden Retrievers are bubbly blonds, not all Rottweilers are protective, not all Basset Hounds are lazy—but there *are* certain traits that you can more or less expect in any given breed. On the other hand, lots of people find mixed breeds charming because of their uniqueness: if

Miles and Molly are all-American mixed breeds—and proud of it!

you adopt a Welsh Corgi–Doberman Pinscher–Pointer–Pekingese mix, you can be pretty sure that there won't be very many more like her in the world!

If you have any intention of registering your dog with the American Kennel Club or showing her in AKC Obedience Trials (see Chapters 6 and 7), she'll have to be an identifiable purebred. But mixed breeds now have their own registry organizations and can be entered in some obedience competitions and mixed-breed dog shows; more doors are opening for them all the time. (See Chapter 7 and Appendix C for information on registering your adopted dog with the appropriate organization.)

Remember that some breeds are much more likely to show up in shelters than others: you won't have much trouble finding a Labrador or a Cocker Spaniel in an adoption facility, but locating a Kerry Blue Terrier or a Komondor will prove somewhat more challenging! If you're eager to adopt a puppy or dog of an uncommon breed, your best bet is to contact a breed rescue society—an organization, usually volunteer-run, devoted to rescuing and finding homes for dogs of a specific breed who have been abandoned or given up by their previous owners. (Appendix A will give you more information about finding breed rescue societies in your area.)

Most of the breeds seen frequently in shelters are "popular" breeds, and that has its advantages and disadvantages. Breeds usually become popular for good reasons: because they're intelligent or friendly or pretty. But when public demand for a particular breed increases suddenly (because the Queen of England has one, or a television show features one), overbreeding results, and careless matings can lead to major physical and temperamental problems. Though most reputable breeders genuinely strive for quality and soundness in the dogs they raise, some "breeders," more interested in capitalizing on a fad than in producing good dogs, have done a lot of damage to some of America's favorite breeds. So when you adopt a dog of one of those breeds, you must be very careful to ensure that she's healthy and sweet-tempered. (Of course, a lot of those "popular" dogs end up in shelters through no shortcomings of their own. Too often, people see a breed on television or in a magazine, decide to get one of their own, and then realize that it isn't the breed for them after all. That's why it's so important not to adopt on impulse!)

In mixed breeds' favor is the phenomenon known as *hybrid vigor*: the hardiness that survives in a species after years of natural selection. It might seem paradoxical that dogs who have lived on the streets, in the woods, and in shelters could be healthier and better-tempered than selectively bred purebreds, but it can be true. Poor breeders like those previously mentioned often produce puppies with regard only to profit rather than to quality, or they may breed dogs in an attempt to cultivate one or two certain characteristics at the expense of others. Nature, though less careful with her breeding, sometimes yields better results. Natural selection does a fair job of weeding out what's unnecessary and harmful and keeping what's useful and beneficial, and the crossing of breeds often cancels out unfavorable genetic traits within each breed.

Purebred or mix? It's up to you. No matter what your dog's family tree looks like, she's going to be a one-of-a-kind.

Boning Up on the Breeds

Maybe you already know exactly what kind of dog you want; perhaps you've had dogs of a particular breed in the past and are completely familiar and enamored with them. But if not, we suggest that you start looking around for breeds or breed mixes that seem to fit the specifications you've been outlining.

A good place to start is at the library or the bookstore. Appendix C lists several books that will give you pictures and descriptions of hundreds of different breeds. Of course, they can't present a complete profile of any breed in one or two pages, but they *can* tell you, for example, which breeds need a lot of exercise or grooming, which ones are particularly gentle with children, or which tend to make good watchdogs. And that can help you formulate a list of breeds that might meet your needs, as long as you read with the understanding that, as we've said, generalizations can be misleading, and there's plenty of variation within every breed.

Even if you've decided you want a mixed breed, this is a smart way to begin your search; after all, every mutt has purebreds in her genealogy, and many will still have identifiable physical and temperamental traits characteristic of the breeds in their backgrounds. So if you decide that you like what you know about German Shepherds, for example, you might want to look for a Shepherd mix when you visit shelters.

Books are a great beginning, but the best way to know what kinds of dogs appeal to you is to go and meet some! Spend time with friends' dogs. Hang around a vet's office or dog training school. Go to a dog show and talk to the exhibitors about their breeds. In short, become as familiar as you can with the breeds or mixes that interest you.

Mixed Breeds: Reading Between the Bloodlines

Suppose you've decided that you definitely want a mixed breed, or you've found that no single breed really floats your boat. You'll have an easier time picking a mutt who fits your "profile" if you can identify the breeds that helped to create her, and if you understand some of the characteristics that they'll probably have contributed to her physical and emotional makeup. After all, a Husky-Collie mix isn't going to look or act like a Poodle-Schnauzer mix, and you'll want to know what to expect from the various mixes you meet as you visit shelters.

Sometimes it's easy to look at a mixed-breed dog and know exactly what her parents were. Usually, though, it's not quite so clear-cut. Most mixes aren't simply crosses of two purebreds; they're the products of one or more generations of mixed breeds, and with every generation, the breeds get more and more muddled together and tougher to discern. Still, smart shelter employees should be able to tell you what breed or breeds have contributed most strongly to the genetic makeup of

Who says you can't find rare breeds in shelters? Chumley, CDX, a Wirehaired Pointing Griffon, was on "death row" at a pound when he was rescued.

almost every shelter dog, and you can use that information to help determine which one might meet your needs.

Every breed of dog was initially developed to perform a specific task or fulfill a specific role. And even if a breed no longer performs its original job, it generally retains the characteristics which made it ideal for that job in the first place, so you can tell a lot about a dog's personality by knowing what's in her gene pool. And you can look for certain kinds of breed mixtures according to which ones seem to fit your preferences best. We can group dogs into several different categories based on their original purposes, and this may help you decide what kind of breed mixture you want. (Again, don't forget that these are only generalizations.)

Sporting dogs were born to hunt. Retrievers (especially Labradors), spaniels (especially Cockers), Pointers and Poodles (yes, they really are sporting dogs!) all show up frequently as shelter dogs, either as pure-breds or in combination with other breeds. All were bred to find, flush or fetch game, which means they'll usually chase tennis balls happily and let you know when a flock of geese flies over your house. More importantly, they've been bred to work closely and enthusiastically with people, so they tend to take well to training and enjoy human company.

Scent hounds are famous for their noses, which they originally used to sniff out small prey. Beagles, Basset Hounds and Dachshunds, to name only a few, still like to press their snouts to the ground and follow a good trail now and then, and that can lead them to want to wander away from home if they're not kept under watch. Hounds tend to be independent, even stubborn at times, and they can be talkative, but they're good-natured and gentle.

Sighthounds were developed to use their eyes to spot prey and their long legs to chase it. Greyhounds, Irish Wolfhounds, Afghan Hounds,

Whippets and the other sighthounds are lean, lanky, speedy dogs with keen vision (but lousy depth perception!). Like their nosy cousins, they tend to be somewhat independent, but they're generally pretty quiet, and they have sweet, even temperaments.

Working dogs comprise a whole range of breeds, most of which were created as protection or service dogs. This group includes rescue dogs like Newfoundlands and Saint Bernards, sled dogs like Alaskan Malamutes and Siberian Huskies and guard dogs like Rottweilers and Doberman Pinschers. Most are large and strong and known for their intelligence and courage. Training them requires firmness, but they're sharp and eager to learn, and they're devoutly loyal to their people.

Herding dogs do just what their name says: they originally rounded up sheep or cattle, but they'll be just as happy to round up your family members and other animals! Collies, Shetland Sheepdogs, German Shepherds and Border Collies are among the breeds designed to keep livestock in line. They're bright, active and trainable, with a tendency to like to keep their family "flocks" together and protected, so if you get a dog with herding breeds in her heritage, be prepared to be rounded into a corner now and then.

Terriers, originally used to hunt small ground-dwelling animals, pack lots of punch into their small- to medium-sized bodies! Most terriers, like Airedales, Miniature Schnauzers, Fox Terriers and West Highland White Terriers (Westies), have short or wiry hair and compact bodies; they're strong-willed, bold, and clever—often even cocky. Training them takes confidence, firmness and a sense of humor!

Toy dogs are saddled with a rather patronizing name, but that doesn't mean these little fellows don't command plenty of respect. These tiny giants—including Toy Poodles, Pomeranians, Pekingese, Maltese and Yorkshire Terriers (Yorkies)—were bred mostly for the purpose of sitting on laps and keeping people company. But they've got plenty of energy and intelligence, and the only real difficulty in training them is their miniature size; people with bad backs should probably steer away from the toy breeds!

Use these distinctions to help yourself decide what kind of mixed breed is the one for you, but remember that they're only a guide. When you see a German Shepherd mix or a Collie-retriever cross in a shelter, you'll have at least some idea of what to expect, but you can be sure that she'll have plenty of personality traits all her own, too!

Bear in mind, too, that genealogy is only one factor in a dog's character. Environment and training have just as much to do with how a dog behaves as parenting does. So just because you want a dog who will play fetch with you, that doesn't mean you have to get a retriever or retriever mix; a herding-type dog can learn to go get a tennis ball just as well, even though it may not come quite as naturally to her.

Finally, we should make some mention of those mutts who fall under the category of "unidentifiable"—or, to put it in a nicer way, "unique!" We've met a handful of dogs who are such odd combinations of features that they defy categorization. But that certainly doesn't stop them from making terrific companions. Chapter 4 will tell you how to discern a lot about a shelter dog's personality even if her heredity is no help.

Onward!

Congratulations—you're well on your way to formulating a strong, but not inflexible, "puppy profile" that will serve you well as you continue your search for your new canine companion. Time to move on to the next step: Finding the right shelter!

SUCCESS STORY #2

Mia Thompson and Kaya
New York, New York

Since early childhood, I wanted a dog. Living in apartments made that an impossibility, until I was twelve and my family moved into a house. Within a week, I'd found out that some neighbors had a litter of puppies, and I was determined to have one. Of course I would be responsible for feeding and walking and training her, and cleaning up the inevitable messes. I convinced my mother that this was a good idea. When Belle first came home at seven weeks old, she was as wide as she was long, and my mother instantly fell in love. Belle was incredibly cute, as I guess all puppies are, but she also knew how to flirt. Today, at twelve, she continues to do so. Every guest in our house witnesses her act: She approaches with a ball in her mouth, shows them her profile and coyly turns her head away when they try to take the ball. She's made it an art.

Two years later, A.J. moved in. At six weeks old, she was already protective, emitting surprisingly feisty little barks whenever she felt we might be in danger. That included everything from the mailman coming to the door to leaves falling off the trees across the street. Today she still keeps long vigils, sitting on the coffee table at our front window with her nose pressed against the glass. Someone's forever cleaning off the snout prints.

Two years after we got A.J., Barney entered the picture. A friend had found Barney in his garage, sleeping in a pile of carpet scraps. But the friend's girlfriend didn't like dogs, so he had to choose, and, crazily, he chose the woman. Barney initially was timid and a fear biter, but after months of patience and love, he settled into his new environment. However, as they say, you can take the dog out of the street, but you can't take the street out of the dog. Despite an abundant supply of perfectly good food at his disposal, Barney still insists on making frequent excursions to various garbage cans in the neighborhood.

The three of them have always been a constant source of amusement, comfort and unconditional love. When I went away to college at Oberlin, I missed that. Visits home were anticipated not because of friends and family but because I'd get to see my dogs. Sure, I missed my friends and family, but I could talk to them on the phone; dogs aren't so good at that (though my mom and I insisted on trying). I missed A.J. waking me up in the morning by licking me in the face and then jumping on me. I missed Barney getting in my lap whenever I sat down (even when I had a plate of food in my lap). I missed Belle's flirting.

During my junior year, when I finally had a place of my own, I decided that the visits weren't enough and I wanted to have a dog with me. I knew I couldn't separate the three at home, since they're very attached to each other. That meant getting another dog. So one afternoon at the end of May, my then-boyfriend and I went to the animal shelter in Oberlin and picked out a puppy. (Theoretically, we were getting this dog together, though I would keep her when he went back to school in Ithaca.) Kaya was more than happy to go home with us. She bonded with us immediately, and we spoiled her like new parents spoil their first child. Over the summer, she went everywhere with us, and especially enjoyed camping. Exploring every inch of the forest floor was exciting for her, as were the random things she discovered and decided were edible (she ate deer droppings like they were Raisinets).

Well, the boy and I went our separate ways, but Kaya is still around. She just turned a year old and still has the energy of a puppy on speed (as I write this, she's tearing around my apartment like a crazed demon, playing with some toy that sounds like mice being tortured). I'm amazed at how much she's grown, physically and otherwise. She knows how to ask for (and get) what she wants; when vocalizing doesn't work, she uses her surprisingly coordinated paws to swat me. We communicate with each other as expressively as I do with many people. She knows when I'm not in the mood, and she knows what to do so that I am.

She's been an enormous responsibility, and I've definitely had to sacrifice things for her—no late nights, no sudden trips. But it's all been worth it. What I get back in amusement, excitement, and pure love far surpasses the spontaneity I've had to suppress. She reminds me of the simple joy that can exist in life—something that, as I grow older, becomes increasingly difficult to find. Whether it's my coming home, or her chasing a stick or running around in circles for no reason other than to run around in circles, Kaya finds a reason to be happy. That's what I love most about her.

She is completely happy chasing rocks. We should all be so lucky.

CHAPTER 3

Shopping for a Shelter

Y ou wouldn't adopt a dog from just anyone, would you? Of course not. You want to feel as though you're adopting your pup from a loving foster home, not rescuing her from a wicked captor. So once you've decided to adopt a special pup, the next important step is finding the right shelter. Not all adoption facilities are created equal, and you'll do yourself and your dog a tremendous service by choosing one that will meet your needs both now and throughout your life together.

As you shelter-shop, remember that you're looking for—ideally—a place with a knowledgeable and caring staff, a comfortable physical setting for its animals and sensible policies and services to help make the adoption process smooth for adopters and dogs alike. It doesn't have to be huge, palatial or wealthy; it just has to do its job thoroughly and conscientiously. Chances are, there's a place like that not far from you. But remember, too, that great doggie companions can turn up where you least expect them, so even if you don't find the perfect shelter in your area, that's no reason to give up your dreams of adoption.

Know Your (Adoption) Options!

What's the difference between a private shelter and a Humane Society, or an SPCA and a pound? The distinctions aren't always crystal-clear, and distinguishing among the different kinds of adoption facilities can get confusing. But in general, shelters, Humane Societies and SPCAs (Societies for the Prevention of Cruelty to Animals) are organizations dedicated to the rescuing and adopting of homeless animals, whereas "pounds" are municipally run animal-control facilities that offer few or no adoption-oriented services.

Most shelters, Humane Societies, and SPCAs are privately operated, self-supported and independent; they care for and adopt abandoned

animals and are often involved in humane education and litigation as well. Pounds, on the other hand, are usually operated under the auspices of a city or county government for the purpose of controlling stray animals. But that's not always the case, so you can find out exactly who operates the shelters *you* visit.

Clearly, some pounds and shelters are better than others. Many facilities really accommodate their residents and work hard to adopt them to good people; some other facilities don't meet their dogs' needs and don't do what it takes to find them homes. Unless you're an experienced dog person and know exactly what you're doing, you'll probably be better off shopping around until you find a shelter or pound that's clean, comfortable, and staffed by interested, knowledgeable people. They'll give you the support and services you need to adopt the right pup and make her transition into your home as smooth as possible.

But remember: Where an abandoned dog ends up is usually just a matter of luck or un-luck. A dog at a posh shelter isn't necessarily a more worthy pup than one at an under-funded city pound. So don't write off the less-impressive adoption facilities altogether; just be sure you're very, very careful and well-informed if you decide to adopt from a shelter or pound that may not be able to give you much help with the adoption process.

Doing Your Homework

In this as in all phases of the adoption process, planning and patience are key! You'll spare yourself time, fatigue and gasoline if you narrow down your shelter options from home. So the first place to turn as you shop for a shelter is your phone book. Look under "Animal Shelters" or "Humane Societies" in your local Yellow Pages. If you have a veterinarian or friends and family members with adopted dogs, ask them to recommend shelters to you. Then sit down with your telephone and a pencil and paper to do a little research.

Keep in mind that shelters are busy and often understaffed places, and they may not have the money to hire full-time receptionists. If you explain in a friendly and concise manner that you're interested in adopting a dog and want to gather as much information as possible, you'll probably find that shelter employees are eager to talk to you, but don't be surprised if some of them seem to be distracted or in a hurry to get back to the animals. If you feel you're being treated rudely or evasively, though, then *you* can be in a hurry to get off the phone and move on to another shelter.

Here's a list of some of the most important questions you should ask—and the answers you want to hear—when you first speak to shelter employees.

"How do you socialize your dogs?"

Shelters don't just feed and house abandoned dogs; they socialize and rehabilitate them, too. At the best facilities, dogs are better-adjusted when they leave than they were when they arrived; at the worst ones, the opposite is true. You don't want to adopt a pup who's been stuck in a cage and ignored ever since arriving at the adoption facility, since whatever behavior or attitude problems she may have had previously won't have improved—and will probably have gotten much worse—during her time at the shelter. And if she hasn't been getting enough human contact, she may have become depressed or withdrawn. So ask how many hours of human contact each shelter's dogs receive daily, how often they get to take walks or bat a ball around, how many different people spend time with them and whether they ever have the chance to play and be goofy with other dogs.

Socialization is especially important if you're looking for a puppy. The early weeks of a dog's life are a crucial formative time, and a puppy who doesn't learn to interact with humans from the start may have lifelong adjustment problems ahead of her. Ask whether the shelter has any special socialization procedures for young puppies.

"Do you evaluate your dogs' temperaments?"

At some shelters, you'll find formal temperament evaluations posted on each dog's cage. At others, you'll find staff members who can tell you all about each dog's personality. Either approach is fine. What's *not* fine is a shelter whose employees know little or nothing about the natures of its animals. Since you'll have only a limited time to spend with the dogs you meet, you'll want to find out about their habits, quirks, assets and drawbacks from the people who have been caring for them.

Ask whether the shelter does any formal temperament testing of its animals (that is, specific exercises designed to assess a dog's level of dominance, submissiveness, protectiveness, etc.). If the answer is no, ask whether the staff has spent enough time with the dogs to know their dispositions and to know what kinds of adoptive homes will likely be best for them.

"What medical care do you provide for your animals?"

There are certain baseline medical needs that *must* be met before you take a dog from a shelter: she needs to have been wormed; her blood needs to have been checked for heartworm (in most areas of the country); and her ears and skin need to have been checked or treated for mites and other parasites. And she needs to have had her first vaccinations for distemper, hepatitis, leptospirosis, parvovirus and parainfluenza (DHLPP), as well as bordetella, coronavirus and (if she's old enough) rabies. Be certain that any shelter you contact provides at least these basic services.

Spaying or neutering, which we'll discuss in more detail in Chapter 7, is another basic medical requirement that a shelter may or may not provide. Many shelters spay or neuter all dogs six months of age or older before they leave the facility, and that's ideal for you. But lots of shelters, understandably, don't have the money to provide such services. Nevertheless, they're acutely aware of the importance of stemming canine overpopulation, so good shelters *always* require adopters to have their dogs spayed or neutered within a reasonable time period after adoption. Some require a deposit, which is refunded upon submission of proof of spaying or neutering, while others give adopters low-cost

The more contact between shelter dogs and shelter staff, the better! It's clear that these volunteers love their job—and these puppies love *them.*

spaying/neutering certificates from area veterinarians or provide low-cost services themselves.

In some areas, it's becoming common practice for shelters to spay or neuter *all* their dogs—even those under the traditional minimum six-month age. Opinions are mixed on this approach to population control. Cities and counties whose shelters alter 100 percent of their animals report a dramatic decrease in the numbers of stray animals on their streets and of animals euthanized in shelters. But some experts believe that medical complications can arise in dogs who are spayed or neutered too young. If you adopt such a dog, make sure she's been operated on by a reputable veterinarian and is certified healthy before you take her home.

Since you're already aware of the necessity of spaying or neutering, the specific way in which a shelter handles the issue isn't of paramount importance. What *is* important is that they handle it in *some* way, since that's a major sign of a responsible shelter.

"What post-adoption services do you offer?"
Some shelters—especially large, well-funded ones—have the resources to offer obedience classes, behavior consulting, veterinary services,

newsletters and question-and-answer sessions to their adopters. That kind of continued support can be a great help to you as you and your new dog adjust to life together. But most shelters don't have the money, space or people-power to do as much for their adopters and their former canine residents as they'd like. That doesn't mean they aren't interested. A good shelter, even if it can't afford to provide an array of amenities itself, may still offer referral services or special discounted deals with local vets and obedience schools and should always be willing to talk with adopters about whatever problems or successes they may have with their dogs.

A few shelters seem to have a "once you've signed the adoption contract, you're on your own" attitude, and these are the ones you want to steer clear of. Choose a shelter that will take an interest in you and your dog now *and* later.

"What is your policy on euthanasia?"

You might want to find out how the shelters you investigate address the problem of seemingly unadoptable animals. Some facilities, known as "no-kill" shelters, keep all their animals for as long as it takes to find them homes. Sound ideal? It can be: Some shelters, especially small ones that aren't strapped with animal-control duties, really go "above and beyond" in their efforts to make their dogs adoptable and to find them great homes. But a no-kill shelter ceases to be humane when it adopts animals to unsuitable homes just to get rid of them, or when it has to turn away adoptable dogs because its cages are filled with unhealthy, unsound, unhappy animals who may never find homes and might be better off euthanized.

On the other hand, a few shelters euthanize too many animals too soon, often because they don't want to spend their time and money to perform simple medical treatments or to help shy or frightened pups gain the confidence they need to make a successful transition into a new home.

Most shelters fall somewhere in the middle: they keep dogs as long as is practical, but eventually they have to decide which ones are least likely to find homes and must be euthanized to make room for new animals. It's terribly sad, but in most places it's the only way to keep the shelter running and the overpopulation problem from getting out of hand.

It's a tricky issue, but in general, the best shelters maintain a realistic and compassionate stance on euthanasia, putting seriously unhealthy and unstable dogs to sleep and working tirelessly to give the rest the second chances they deserve.

"Do you allow adopters to return dogs with medical or other problems?"

Most reputable shelters will let you return an adopted dog within a certain period of time (usually a week or so) and will refund your adoption fee if a veterinarian diagnoses a previously undiscovered major health problem. Some will do the same if you find that she simply can't stay with you for some unforeseen reason (aggressiveness that hadn't surfaced before, perhaps, or *unreasonable* difficulty adapting to your family, other pets, or living situation). That doesn't mean, obviously, that you ought to adopt with the attitude that you can "exchange" your dog if everything isn't just hunky-dory from day one. These return policies are only for dogs with serious and uncorrectable problems, and they mustn't be abused.

"What do you require of a potential adopter?"

The next section will cover the sorts of questions you're likely to be asked when you visit a shelter to adopt a dog, but you can find out a few basics now. For starters, what adoption fee does the shelter charge and what care and services does that fee include? Remember that a $10 adoption price is no bargain when it covers little or no medical care, while a $50 to $70 fee (which is pretty common in most areas) is a terrific deal if it includes immunizations, spaying or neutering and perhaps a starter kit of information and supplies.

Does the shelter have strict, inflexible rules about who may adopt a dog, or does it evaluate each case individually? Depending on your circumstances, you may run into trouble if you try to adopt from a shelter that absolutely won't release dogs to people who

Knowledgeable, friendly, attentive staff members are one sign of a well-run shelter.

live in apartments or who are under a certain age, for example. Though such regulations may seem infuriatingly arbitrary, they're usually made and enforced for good reasons, as we'll discuss. But if you *know* that you'll be able to give a dog a good home despite an unorthodox living situation, you'll have to find a shelter that's willing to work with you.

"When can I come for a visit?"
Some shelters welcome walk-ins all the time, while others may ask you to make an appointment. If you like what you've heard so far, then by all means find out when you can come and get better acquainted with the employees and the animals!

See for Yourself!
Now it's time to see first-hand the shelters that have passed your phone interview. Before you zoom off to the places on your list, though, please vow to yourself (and make the rest of your family vow, too, if they're coming along) that these will be look-but-don't-touch visits. This isn't the part of the story where you fall hopelessly in love with a puppy or dog, brush aside your better judgment, chuck aside your copy of *The Adoption Option* and whisk her home with you to live happily ever after. We know that's easier said than done, but if you adopt too hurriedly from a shelter you haven't checked out thoroughly, you could be in for trouble later.

Your purpose during this initial visit is to evaluate how well-kept and well-run the facility is. Start with the obvious: Is the shelter an inviting place? Is it clean and well-lit, or is it dingy and dim? Are the employees friendly, interested and willing and able to answer your questions? Do they greet you and offer their assistance, or do they ignore you or seem anxious for you to leave?

Introduce yourself as a potential adopter and ask whether you can see the kennels where the puppies and dogs live. (The staff may want to ask you some questions before you meet the dogs; the next section will tell you what to expect of this casual interview.) And prepare to have your senses assaulted: The smells, sounds and sights of the inside of an animal shelter can be a little overwhelming at first.

Look around. Are the kennels clean? You shouldn't see more than a couple dogs sitting in cages with feces or urine on the floor. (Make allowances, of course, for the fact that dogs aren't always the tidiest animals in the world, and even the most fastidious shelter can't keep all

This is the humble but successful OASIS Animal Shelter—proof that bigger isn't necessarily better when it comes to adoption facilities.

the cages spotless all the time.) Even a clean shelter is probably going to smell like, well, dogs, but if the odor of the place is enough to make your stomach turn, that may be a sign that the cages haven't been disinfected recently or thoroughly enough.

Do the dogs have ample room to stretch their legs? They should at least have room to stand up and walk around a bit. There shouldn't be more than one dog in a single pen, except in the cases of puppies or littermates, and sick animals shouldn't be housed alongside healthy ones. Check the floors of the kennels: Do the dogs have clean bedding to lie on, fresh water to drink and toys to play with? Is there an outdoor area where the dogs can romp?

Most importantly, do the animals look healthy and happy? Are they well-fed and groomed, energetic, and eager to interact with you as you pass their cages, or do they lie listlessly, with dull fur, glazed runny eyes, sores on their skin or deep coughs? Every shelter is likely to have one or two depressed or unfriendly residents, of course, but if you see miserable dog after miserable dog, you might well suspect that this isn't the best place for you to find a chipper canine friend.

Watch the shelter staff members interact with the animals. You'll be able to tell whether they really know and love the dogs or whether they're just feeding and walking them because it's their job. They should be able to talk to you intelligently about the characteristics of the different pups, but they shouldn't be too eager to "make a sale." You want them to be as careful about this adoption as you're going to be; if they seem to want you to pick a dog, any dog, and take her home with you right away, then they aren't looking out for their dogs' welfare or for yours. Shelters that are too hasty in their matchmaking aren't responsible shelters.

It's important to remember that a well-kept, well-run shelter doesn't have to be a big, snazzy shelter. There are lots of small, no-frills adoption facilities—some that are entirely volunteer-operated—which are great places to adopt despite being financially challenged or physically unspectacular. In fact, small shelters with volunteer staffs (we might call them "labor of love" shelters) often know their animals more intimately than large shelters can, and they usually have the time and interest to give every dog and adopter lots of attention. What matters isn't whether a shelter has fancy displays and silver doggie dishes, but whether it has clean facilities, an interested and informed staff and reasonable adoption policies and procedures.

When you visit a shelter, you won't be the only one taking notes and making evaluations; they'll be checking you out, too. Now don't be nervous. This doesn't have to be like meeting your in-laws for the first time. But be aware that adoption is a two-way deal, and the staff members of a really responsible shelter will probably have as many questions for you as you have for them. Be impressed rather than intimidated by their interest, even if their queries occasionally seem nosy or irrelevant. And answer honestly, not defensively or apologetically; after all, you're an intelligent, thoughtful, trustworthy adopter with nothing to hide. The shelter employees aren't trying to trick you or trip you up. Remember, the more they know about you and your lifestyle, the better equipped they'll be to help you pick the right pup when the time comes.

Some shelters will ask you (either during this preliminary visit or when you return looking for a dog) to fill out a written "pre-adoption" form before they'll even show you their dogs. These forms aren't binding; they just help the staff get to know you and your needs. Other shelters have "counseling rooms" where staff members will sit and talk with you before taking you to see their animals. Most shelters will simply interview you informally throughout your visit.

In any case, the basic questions you'll be asked will be pretty much the same, and if you've done your homework thus far, they shouldn't come as surprises. Some of the most common questions are explained in the next sections.

"What kind of dog are you looking for?"

Might as well start right out with a biggie. You, of course, will be well-prepared to answer this question, since you've already formulated your Puppy Profile and can tell the staff members what sort of pup you want and why. Be thorough but flexible; as you chat, the staff may come up with new ideas for you, or they may be able to spot potential problems in your profile and suggest adjustments. Don't let them talk you into anything you don't want, but *do* let their knowledge guide you.

"What are your living quarters like?"

The staff needs to know, for example, whether you live in a big house or a tiny apartment or something in between, so that they can help you find a dog of an appropriate size and energy level. They'll be wary of adopting, say, a big, active dog to a family that lives in a twentieth-story apartment, so if you're interested in getting a dog who might seem unsuited to your living environment, you'll have to convince them that you can make it work.

They'll also need to know whether you rent or own your home. If you're a renter, now is a good time to show proof that you're allowed to have a canine roommate: either a copy of a lease with a "pets allowed" provision, or a signed statement from your landlord.

"Do you have a fenced yard?"

If the answer is "no," don't feel bad; just explain to the staff that you understand that your dog will need exercise and outdoor play, and that you intend to walk her and have fun in the sun (or rain or snow) with her regularly. Tell the staff whether you have—or plan to build—an outdoor pen or kennel for your dog. And if you have special outdoor interests that you'll be sharing with your new dog (hiking or jogging, for example), those, too, can make the absence of a fenced yard less of a drawback.

Even if the answer is "yes," let them know that your fence is high enough and secure enough to confine the kind of dog you want, and that the yard provides adequate shelter from the sun, hot or cold temperatures and precipitation. And be *sure* the staff understands that you're not going to leave your new dog by herself in the yard all day long.

"Are you looking for an indoor or an outdoor dog?"

You already know that there is no such thing as an "outdoor dog." No responsible shelter will adopt a dog to someone who intends to keep her outside all the time. Assure the staff that your dog will be a beloved member of your family, and that you're going to teach her to live comfortably and considerately in the house with you.

"Do you have any children?"

The staff needs to know how many children you have and how old they are. A good shelter won't want to place a fragile, shy or easily irritable puppy or dog into a family with very young members, and they'll probably be able to tell you whether any of their dogs are particularly well-suited to living with children. They also want to be certain that your child-rearing responsibilities won't leave you too exhausted to take care of a dog, and that your little ones understand that they won't be able to pull the new pup's tail or snatch her toys. Explain to the staff members that you've discussed all aspects of dog care with your kids, and you're positive that they're mature and responsible enough to treat a new dog gently and respectfully.

"Who else lives with you?"

This question helps the shelter better understand your living situation and determine whether any conflicts are likely to arise. If you're an adult and you answer "my parents," the staff will want to be sure that you don't adopt a dog who will be rowdy or impatient with older people. If you're a teenager and you answer "my parents," they'll want to be sure that your folks know what you're up to!

Some shelters have policies against adopting dogs to unmarried cohabiting couples or to groups of unrelated people living together. This can become a sticky and frustrating issue, but you need to be prepared to address it if you're in such a situation. Try to see the other side of the issue: Understand that shelters with rules like this are only trying to keep their dogs from getting shafted when couples break up or group homes disband. Too often, when living arrangements change and people move on to different places, no one's willing to take the dog along and she ends up being returned to the shelter or abandoned. In homes with lots of people living together, a dog can get lost in the shuffle, or confusion can arise over whose turn it is to feed or walk her, who's supposed to pay her vet bills and who's going to be in charge of training her. Shelters have seen it happen over and over, and some of them have simply put an end to all such adoptions, to be safe.

Rightly or wrongly, if shelter employees are unwilling to adopt a dog to you because you and your partner are not married or legally recognized as domestic partners, it will be up to you to convince them that your relationship is committed and unlikely to change in the near future—and that if you *do* go your separate ways, one of you will promise to keep and care for the dog. If you live with a group of friends, you'll need to assure the shelter that *everyone* in the household has agreed to the acquisition of a dog (that is, no one's going to have an allergy attack or throw a tantrum because you bring home a puppy as a surprise). And even if everyone is going to help raise the pup, one person in the group should assume primary responsibility for her and plan to take care of her if the group doesn't stay together.

We've known a number of loving, deserving people who had trouble adopting dogs because of policies like these (as well as a few *undeserving* people who, mercifully, were prevented from getting dogs by these same rules). But those who were patient, calm and dedicated all managed to find sympathetic shelters and adopt great dogs. If you demonstrate that you're ready and able to give a dog a loving home, you shouldn't have too much difficulty locating a shelter that will trust you!

"Who will bear the main responsibility of caring for the dog?"

There's one flat-out wrong answer to this question, and you can probably guess what it is. That's right: "the kids!" As we've already discussed, dog care is a duty for adults or mature teenagers, and shelters will be loath to adopt a pup to anyone who doesn't understand that. Even if your kids are going to play a big part in your dog's upbringing (and there's *nothing* wrong with that), the shelter needs to know that *you* will be supervising her and paying for her expenses.

When it's time to take your dog to obedience school, one person needs to become her primary educator (more on educated canines in Chapter 6). If you've already decided who that will be, tell the staff members, and they'll be duly impressed by your forethought.

"Does anyone in the family have allergies?"

People are always bringing dogs to adoption facilities with the explanation, "I can't keep her—my kids are allergic." Sometimes it's true; sometimes it's just a handy excuse. But in any case, shelters are careful about adopting dogs to sneezy people. If you have family members with dog-fur allergies, tell the staff so, and they can probably help you find a dog with a coat that won't shed too much. And if you've taken steps to alleviate the allergy problem (pills, shots), the shelter will know that you're serious about making the situation work.

"What other animals (if any) live with you?"

Go on—tell them all about your other four-legged buddies! They'll probably want to know the species, age, gender, size, breed and temperament of any other dog or cat living in your household. This will help the shelter determine what kind of dog will best get along with your furry family members.

"Are your other animals spayed or neutered?"

Many shelters won't adopt a dog to someone with an unaltered dog at home—mostly for practical reasons, and partly on principle. If you have a grown dog who is not yet spayed or neutered, tell the staff that you intend to correct that situation before you introduce another canine into the household. Then do it!

"What will you do with the dog if you move?"

An easy one for foresighted you: You'll take her with you!

"Have you had dogs in the past, and where are they now?"

It may seem like an odd question, but shelter employees can tell a lot from an answer like "I had two dogs who died of natural causes at thirteen and fifteen years old," as opposed to, say, "I had a dog that ran away and two cats that I gave to a family on a farm when I moved." A good "track record" with dogs can indicate that you're an experienced and committed dog lover who's likely to give a new dog a terrific home.

But shelter folks understand that accidents happen and people make mistakes. Even well-loved and well-supervised dogs get lost, stolen or hit by cars. If you've lost pets under unfortunate circumstances in the past, be honest about it; if you've made mistakes but learned from them, tell the shelter employees so. They're not interested in judging you; they just want to make sure you'll take good care of the dog you adopt.

What if you've never had a dog of your own before? Well, everyone has to start somewhere, and your inexperience doesn't have to be a disadvantage. If you've ever helped care for someone else's dog or worked with animals (at a vet's office or an animal shelter, for instance), those are strong points in your favor. And at the very least, you can tell the staff that you've been reading up on the subject of dog adoption and dog care! (Take a look at Appendix C if you need to bolster your booklist a bit.)

Those are a lot of questions, to be sure, but you can understand why they're all necessary and important. A shelter that cares enough to find out about you and your lifestyle will care enough to help you find a great dog. So don't be annoyed if you feel like you're getting the third degree, and for heaven's sake don't be dishonest. If you're tempted to say "No, of course my son doesn't have allergies" just because he *really* wants that fluffy puppy who's shedding in the corner cage, think about how you'll all feel a few months later when you have to bring the not-so-cute-or-adoptable-anymore puppy back to the shelter because all your vacuuming and brushing isn't enough to keep the sneezes at bay. Just be forthright and friendly, and the shelter staff should do the same.

Home Checks

Some shelters—usually big, well-funded ones with plenty of staff members—have begun to pay visits to the homes of all potential adopters, in much the same way that human service organizations visit families who want to adopt children. Sadly, lots of people lie about their living conditions in order to adopt dogs, so shelters, to their credit, are being extra-careful these days.

Don't be surprised or offended if the shelter employees ask to make a trip to your home, and don't feel that you need to hide anything; they're coming not to pass judgments on your decor, but simply to en-sure that you've got the space and the facilities to keep the kind of dog you want, and that your living quarters are clean enough for a pup. Just show them that you're a responsible housekeeper, and that you have room to accommodate a pup, and you'll be fine.

The Adoption Contract

Most adopters never lay eyes on an actual adoption contract until they've already picked out the dog they want to take home. Why not ask to see a copy of the adopter's agreement now, while you're still checking out shelters? That way, you'll know exactly what you're getting into, and when it really *is* time to adopt, you won't be tempted to skim it and sign it in a rush just so you can hurry home with your new dog!

Adoption contracts come in different breeds, but most of them are really pretty much alike. When you sign an adoption agreement, you promise to provide for your dog's physical and emotional needs through-out her life. You promise to take her to a vet promptly, and to have her vaccinated regularly and spayed (or him neutered) if necessary. In most cases—and this is probably the most widely ignored clause on adoption

If you're searching for a purebred like Macduff, a West Highland White Terrier, check out breed rescue societies as well as shelters.

contracts—you promise to bring her back to this particular shelter if you someday find that you really can't keep her.

The Final Cut

You've called shelters on the phone, driven around visiting them for a weekend, taken copious notes, and answered more questions than a game-show contestant. By now, you probably have a pretty good idea of which shelters make you feel comfortable and welcome—which ones make you *want* to adopt one of their dogs. These are the places where you'll start your search for the right dog. If you already feel great about the shelters you've seen, and you're pretty sure you can find a great pup at one of them, then turn straight to Chapter 4 and let the fun begin!

But suppose you're not convinced. Maybe you liked the shelters, but you didn't see any dogs that looked like the kind you want. If you're interested in adopting a dog of a particular breed, and you don't think you'll be able to find one in a shelter, then it's probably time to look into breed rescue societies—organizations, usually under the auspices of breed clubs, which provide foster care and find permanent homes for abandoned dogs of that breed. Or you might be interested in adopting a retired racing dog. Appendix A can help you locate a pup through these channels.

Maybe your heart is set on a shelter dog, but you didn't find a shelter with the inviting facilities and helpful staff you'd hoped for. Don't give up. Some folks are lucky enough to have spiffy, responsible, generously endowed shelters near them, and some aren't. Sure, a well-run shelter can make the adoption process a lot more simple and secure, but if you've done your homework and are careful—and we know that you have and you are!—you can find yourself a delightful dog even without that kind of support. So be patient and optimistic, and have fun picking the pup for you!

SUCCESS STORY #3

Jackie and Harris Ordelheide and Lucy
St. Charles, Missouri

I've been volunteering with the St. Charles Humane Society ever since January of 1988, when we opened a small no-kill adoption facility in a blue three-room house in old St. Charles. Over the years, I've cleaned cages, transported animals to the veterinarian's office, answered the telephones and brought home the dirty laundry every day for several months until some kind person donated a washer and dryer to the pet adoption center. I've made follow-up calls to adopters to make sure they've had their pets spayed or neutered (though that job has been eliminated now that we spay or neuter all our animals before they leave the premises). Harris and I have helped prepare the quarterly newsletter for mailing for the past five years. And on November 16, 1988, we found Lucy.

Lucy's previous owners brought her to the pet adoption center when she was a year old; they had a baby and worked all day, and they decided they couldn't take care of the red long-haired Dachshund anymore. So she suddenly found herself in a big chain-link cage at the back of the little animal shelter.

People came and looked at her and talked to her, but they passed her by; they wanted a puppy, not a year-old dog, even though Lucy did her best to tell them that she'd be easy to housebreak, she wouldn't chew things and she'd give them lots of love. Lucy was beginning to grow very sad when I took an interest in her. I'd had a short-haired Dachshund before, and I loved the breed. And, as Harris said, adopting a grown dog rather than a puppy was like buying a demonstration car as opposed to a new one: she'd had some use, but the bugs had been taken care of!

Lucy has brought much pleasure into our lives. When she joined our family, she taught us several new tricks—among them, her ability to wrap us completely around her paw without even working up a sweat! She wasn't housebroken at first, but she was so eager to please us that it didn't take long for her to catch on. Lucy's a little ham who loves cuddling and giving kisses; she's an all-around angel, and not a fussy eater, as she proved by eating one of Harris's hearing aids to the tune of six hundred dollars.

And Lucy loves her siblings. She has a big brother, Charley Brown, who's a lovable Dachshund–Lhasa Apso mix; they romp, talk, walk, play and sleep together. And she has a feline sister, Twinkle Toes, who was a stray who came to eat at our house at night (we could always spot her by her white feet in the dark). I took her to the adoption center to find her a new home, but I missed her so much that I ended up going back and adopting her myself. Twink was lean and lonely when she first came home, but now she's an eighteen-pound, contented fat cat who loves to lie on her back and have her tummy rubbed.

As for Lucy, she's a joy; what more can I say! The St. Charles Humane Society, where I still volunteer, has moved to a bigger facility now, but our goal is still the same: to help God's little creatures, like Lucy, in every way that we can.

CHAPTER 4

Picking the Pup for You

"Enough!" you're probably thinking by now. "No more plotting and planning! I want a dog already!"

But you know what they say: Adopt in haste and repent at leisure. Keep the faith; your hard work is going to pay off very soon. Now that you've thought about what kind of puppy or dog you want, and you've found one or more shelters you trust, it's time to get down to brass tacks and get yourself a great friend.

But don't get mushy now! It's easy, very easy, to go to the shelter, lock eyes with some sweet pooch, and let all your planning and practicality ooze right out your fingertips. Don't let that happen. You owe it to yourself and your new dog to choose carefully and intelligently, and that's what this chapter will help you do. After all, you wouldn't buy a car without going to different dealers and test-driving different models, and the commitment you make to a dog is certainly more important, and probably longer-lasting, than the commitment you make to a car!

It bears repeating that you are probably *not* going to find any single dog that fulfills every one of your wishes. (That's another difference between cars and dogs: dogs don't come with option packages!) And no matter how perfect a dog you find, you can look forward to some hectic and perhaps frustrating times as she gets used to her new life with you. But if you've done your homework, and if you know what to look for in the dogs you encounter, you're going to make one special pup very happy—and vice versa!

Try very hard *not* to fall in love with every puppy or dog you see. You cannot take them all home (repeating for those of you with especially generous souls: *You cannot take them all home!*), and you can't afford to feel guilty about the ones you have to leave behind. We don't even recommend that you take two dogs at once; it's smarter to start with one and add another later if you want to. The more die-hard a dog

lover you are, the tougher it is to go to an animal shelter and not want to rescue every critter in the place, but remind yourself that you're there to find one terrific dog, not to start your own canine commune.

For all our hard-hearted rules and regulations about dog adoption, by the way, we're not completely unsentimental. We know that sometimes our instincts can override our best-laid plans. So what should you do if, after you've visited a couple of shelters and met a variety of dogs, the dog you really want isn't anything like the one you'd set out to find? Don't just gather her into your arms and dash off into the sunset, but don't necessarily write her off, either. For example, if you're looking for a short-haired toy dog and you fall in love with a big, woolly pooch, consider very carefully whether you can give her what she needs, and whether she can fit comfortably into your home and your schedule. If you're doubtful, it's best not to make any promises to her, because you'll both be miserable if things don't work out and you have to bring her back to the shelter. But if your honest answer is "yes," and if you're willing to make some adjustments for her, then we'd hardly try to talk you out of adopting the dog you adore!

What if, on the other hand, you make the rounds of the shelters near you and you don't find a dog who truly "clicks" with you? Don't feel pressured to adopt one who doesn't feel right. When it comes to adoption, for better or worse, there are lots of fish in the sea; wait a week or so and go back to the shelters until you find the one you want to take home with you!

All right, then, without further ado, let's find a dog!

Step 1: Timing is Everything

When is the best time to get a dog? Well, perhaps we should start by listing some of the worst times:

- Before or during a hectic holiday season;
- Just before you leave for a vacation;
- When (or before) you have houseguests;
- At the beginning of a school year, if you have children;
- At the peak of a very hot summer or a very cold winter;
- Any time you're especially busy or stressed out!

If you can arrange for a few days off from work, that's an ideal time to introduce a new dog to the household. The more you can be at home and at leisure during your first days and weeks with your dog, the less bumpy your adjustment period will be, and the more time you'll have to get to know your new friend.

If you have kids, they'll probably want to be around too, so summertime is prime adoption season, provided you're not planning to leave town for a trip anytime very soon. The dead of winter is a less terrific time, since your new dog is going to need plenty of walking and exercising as she becomes housebroken.

In general, pick a time when you're feeling at least relatively relaxed and un-stressed. The addition of a dog to the family should be *fun*—not just another hassle!

Step 2: Go Prepared!

There are a few things you need to remember to pack into your car before you head for the shelter:

Your puppy profile. There's no sense in making a shopping list if you leave it at home when you go to the grocery store, so don't forget to bring along the notes you've made for yourself about what kind of dog you want! It's easy to let all the smart decisions you've made slip out of your mind if you don't have them on paper in front of you.

A pen and paper. You're going to meet a lot of dogs, and writing down a little bit about the ones who interest you will help you keep them straight. You'll want to be able to consider your choices when you're at home, away from the shelter; keeping records of the dogs you've seen will allow you to do that.

Comfortable clothes. Remember, it's a dog shelter, not a cocktail party, so dress appropriately! You're going to be getting down and at least a little bit dirty with dogs who may not have had a bath recently and who may not know that they shouldn't jump or climb on you; accordingly, don't wear anything that you couldn't bear to see paw-printed or drooled on. Jeans are a good bet; they'll also keep your legs protected in case you get scratched or nipped at by a pup. Wear comfy shoes, too, so that you can walk around with ease.

Bring along as many members of your household as possible. Singles need not worry, but if you have family members or roommates who will be living with a new dog, they should also be involved in her selection. That might seem ridiculously obvious, but we've known many, many people who have adopted dogs and then returned them because "the kids didn't get along with her" or "she didn't like my in-laws." You shouldn't necessarily let children, especially young ones, influence your decision too much, but you at least need to be sure that they'll get along with and not be afraid of the dog you choose. By the way, *don't* bring any other dogs or pets along with you unless you have permission from the shelter to do so. Most shelters don't allow outside dogs on their premises because of the risk of dog fights or disease transmission.

Time. Well, it's not exactly something you can pack into your car, but it's certainly important. Leave yourself enough time—probably at least a couple hours—so that you won't feel hurried as you talk to shelter employees and get to know a handful of dogs. If finding a few free hours to go shelter-visiting feels like a strain on your schedule, then you may want to ask yourself whether you're really going to have enough time for a dog.

A good attitude. Patience, cheer and a sense of humor will serve you well during the adoption process—and you may as well start practicing them now, since you'll need them aplenty during the rest of your life with your dog!

Step 3: First Impressions

Write this at the top of your puppy profile: "I will not adopt a dog from the first shelter I visit!" You want to check out all your choices before

Allow plenty of time to talk, and let the shelter staff help you make the best possible choice.

you pick out your special dog, and you'll want some time to think about them away from the hectic atmosphere of the shelter.

Now that you've strengthened your resolve, head to one of the shelters on your short list and get to know its people and dogs! Introduce yourself to the employees or volunteers if they don't already know you from your previous visit. Tell them what you're looking for. Tell them a little bit about your family and your living situation. Let them know that you're serious about finding a great puppy or dog, and they'll be serious in their attempts to help you out.

Perhaps you've already answered their questions about your lifestyle and your plans for this dog on your first visit (see Chapter 3); if not, prepare to do that now. Again, don't be offended by what may seem like nosy or irrelevant questions. Be friendly and answer honestly. Understand that the shelter people are only trying to find the best possible homes for their dogs, and if you've done your homework, you've got nothing to worry about.

Next, since you can't get acquainted with every single dog in the shelter, narrow down your options. Take a look around and see which dogs look like good prospects. Share your list of desires and needs with a shelter employee; ask him or her to show you a number of dogs who might fit the bill. Remember, first impressions count—but don't overlook the "dark horses" in favor of the flashier or cuter dogs! How a dog looks or acts from behind her cage door may not accurately reflect her personality; the only way to find out what a dog's really made of is to get to know her, and that's what Steps 4A and 4B (so numbered because they really need to be done simultaneously) are all about.

Step 4A: Run a Background Check

Now that the shelter has checked you out, it's *your* turn to do some checking up! One of the best ways to find out about the dogs who interest you is to talk to the shelter employees. After all, you picked this shelter because its people seemed knowledgeable, interested and friendly, and now is the time to let their experience guide you in your selection. Knowing what questions to ask about the dogs you meet is crucial. Here's a list—by no means exhaustive—to get you started; ask these questions about each dog who intrigues you, and don't forget to write down the answers you get. (Some or most of this information may already be answered for you if the dogs' cages have information cards or evaluation sheets on them; read carefully whatever appears on each dog's "rap sheet," but talk to the employees anyway, as they can give you more insights than a piece of paper can!)

Is the dog a male or a female? Don't be embarrassed if you have to ask; sometimes it's hard to tell!

How old is she? This, too, is important information that may not be immediately obvious. Of course, the shelter workers may not be able to give you an exact age, but they can probably make an educated guess.

What breed or breed mixture is she? As we've noted, this can often tell you something about how she'll behave. Again, you may not get a precise answer, since the heritage of most shelter dogs is almost impossible to know for certain, but you can probably find out what breed or breeds have contributed predominantly to her makeup, and you can combine that information with the general guidelines in Chapter 2's "Boning Up on the Breeds" section to make some conjectures about her character and her tendencies.

Where did she come from? Was she picked up by the highway? Found in a barn? Abandoned by a dumpster? If so, find out what condition (physical and emotional) she was in when she came to the shelter. Or was she brought to the shelter by the people with whom she previously lived? If that's the case, find out why they gave her up. But keep in mind that lots of people lie—or at least *exaggerate*—about why they leave their dogs at shelters. The standard reasons given are "The children are allergic" or "We're moving and can't take her with us," and while those may indeed be valid sometimes, the truth is often that the dog has had behavior problems which the people don't want to address (or even that they inadvertently caused) and are embarrassed to admit. Be aware, too, that when a dog's cage card or rap sheet says, for instance, that she "couldn't be housebroken" or "wouldn't stop jumping," that usually means that her previous people just didn't know how to solve her problems or didn't try hard enough. So don't believe everything you read.

Does she have any bad habits? You need to know whether this dog is a persistent jumper, chewer or barker, and you need to know just how serious the problem is. If she's been known to bite, for example, you'll probably be better off with another dog. If, on the other hand, she just tends to get overenthusiastic and leap up on people when she greets them, that's a problem you can work with. Every dog is likely to have a couple of bad habits that you'll need to help her break, but don't try to be a hero by adopting the dog with the most horrible behavior problems in the shelter.

If she's a small puppy, what has her infancy been like? Was she properly nursed by her mother until an appropriate age (at least five or six weeks, and preferably seven), or was she separated from her mother and the rest of her litter too young (which could lead to problems with adjusting to adult life and accepting authority)? If she came to the shelter with her entire litter, find out how she relates to her siblings: is she a bossy puppy, or does she let the others walk all over her?

How does she interact with shelter workers? This is another biggie. The shelter employees and volunteers have spent time socializing and entertaining this dog, and they know her personality better than anyone else. Find out whether she's trusting or reserved, solitary or sociable, playful or serious, silent or garrulous, quick-witted or slow to learn, slobbery or tight-lipped. What games does she like? How much affection does she demand? Does she know any words or commands? Is she accustomed to walking on a leash? You can tell a lot by listening to how the employees talk about a dog; do they seem to like her and enjoy spending time with her?

How does she interact with children? If this dog has been visited by families with children, has she been trustworthy and tolerant around them? You might also try to find out whether she previously lived in a home with young people and whether she had any problems getting along with them.

How does she interact with other dogs? Even if *you* don't have any other dogs, your friends and neighbors probably do, so you don't want to adopt a dog who's going to be aggressive toward them (or terrified of them!). Ask whether she tends to be dominant or submissive toward the other canines she encounters, whether she knows how to play appropriately with them and whether she's ever lived with other animals before.

How active is she? Does she crave lots of exercise and run around her cage in circles, or is she content to stay sedentary and just stretch her legs now and then? Keep in mind, of course, that some dogs tend to get a little listless and less active in a shelter, while others become more hyper when they're in a cage, so you can't always trust that the activity level you see will be the activity level you get!

Is she healthy? Find out whether she's had any medical problems before or since her arrival at the shelter. That might include anything from fleas to heartworm; you deserve to know exactly what troubles she's had, what's been done about them and whether she'll need any further treatment. It's not uncommon for shelter dogs to have contracted illnesses or sustained injuries during their pre-shelter days, but you probably don't want to take on the responsibility of a dog who has health problems that may linger and drain your money and time.

How has she changed since arriving at the shelter? This is a critical question that's not asked frequently enough. You're not only interested in how a dog acts today; you want to know how she adapts to situations, how quickly she learns and adjusts, how she responds to socialization and attention. Ask how she acted when she first came to the shelter as compared to her demeanor now. Have her behavior and attitude changed for the better or for the worse? Some dogs grow depressed and even unfriendly after long shelter stays (although this shouldn't happen very often in good shelters, where employees are careful to give them plenty of attention). On the other hand, some of our favorite and most successful shelter residents have been dogs who started out inauspiciously, to say the least! Consider Autumn Joy, a terrified and emaciated Shepherd mix who called a barn home until we lured her out over a three-day period. She spent a week shivering and cowering when anyone looked at her or reached toward her, but by the time she was adopted a month later, she was as ebullient and well-adjusted as any dog in the shelter, thanks to her resilient character and some careful socialization.

How much time does she have left? Unless the shelter has a no-kill policy, each dog may have a deadline by which she must be adopted or be euthanized. We don't encourage you to adopt a dog just because her time is almost up, but if you have to decide between two dogs, you might feel better taking the one whose chances are slimmer. And you need to be sure that you won't come back to the shelter in a day or two and find the dog you liked gone.

Don't be limited by this list; feel free to ask anything you want to know. But don't put the shelter people in an awkward position by asking them questions so specific or so obscure that they can't possibly give you a satisfactory answer. It's fine to ask approximately how large a puppy will grow to be, but don't expect to get an exact poundage. Ask how she relates to other animals, but don't expect to be told definitely whether she'll get along with your cat or guinea pig at home. Remember, shelter employees are experienced "dog people" who can give you their educated opinions and predictions, but they generally don't claim to be psychics.

When you ask questions of the shelter employees or volunteers, trust the answers you receive. If you hear a preponderance of "I don't knows," you may want to check with another employee, but an occasional one is to be expected since there's always an element of mystery to a shelter dog. However, if you feel that the shelter workers are being deliberately misleading or evasive, get thee to another shelter, pronto!

Step 4B: Get a Little Closer!

Talking to the people who know her best is one key way to get a feel for a dog and her compatibility with you. The other key way is, of course, to spend time with her yourself.

When you've picked out a few dogs who seem to meet your needs, ask whether you can take them away from the others one at a time in order to get better acquainted with them—preferably in a room or outdoor enclosure where you can evaluate each dog individually and make some observations. Bring your family, a shelter worker and your memo pad with you, and get ready to have a little fun!

Put yourself down on her level! This little Shepherd mix is happy to play with a potential adopter.

First, if you haven't done so already, instruct your children not to get too excited about the dogs and puppies they're going to meet. Even kids who don't mean to be rough can sometimes startle a new dog and provoke a nip or a bite by reaching out too suddenly or shouting too loudly. It's best if they hang back for a few minutes and then introduce themselves very slowly and gently to each dog.

Give yourself at least fifteen or twenty minutes with each pup, and remember that when she first emerges from her cage, she's going to need a few minutes to get used to you. She may be in a frenzy at first, happy to be out of her cage and excited to see someone new, and it may take a little while for her to settle down. Or, if she's a bit worried and shy at first, she may need some time to get used to you and come out of her shell. (Of course, if she's still either annoyingly hyper or painfully timid after fifteen minutes, she'd probably have somewhat of a difficult time adjusting to you and to life outside the shelter, and you'll probably want to direct your attentions toward other dogs.)

Start by taking a good look at her. Does she give a general impression of good health? Is her coat dull, dry and patchy, or is it full and shiny? (Remember that a dirty coat can sometimes masquerade as an unhealthy coat, so a good bath may make her look a whole lot better!) Is the skin underneath pink and smooth, or does it have flakes or sores? Check her eyes: they should be clear and bright, not cloudy or runny. Feel her nose: it doesn't have to be cold and wet, but it shouldn't be cracked or crusty. Finally, lift up her lips (or, better yet, ask one of the shelter people to do it for you) and look at her mouth. The gums should be pink, not grey or black, and the teeth should be intact and not too yellowed. (Steal a glance at her tail, too. If it's still wagging after your once-over, score extra points for this pup!)

There are a few simple "tests" you can perform in order to tell much about a puppy's or dog's temperament rather quickly. They aren't pass-or-fail affairs, and they aren't meant to distinguish "good" dogs from "bad" ones, but they *will* help you know what to expect from each dog's behavior and dominance level, and that can make your decision a lot clearer. One person should do the "testing," and another can take notes on the results.

Testing a Puppy

First of all, play with her! Sit on the floor so that you're a friendly, non-threatening figure, and talk to her in a sweet voice; let her come to you, climb into your lap, sniff you, get used to your presence. Use a toy or a treat to break the ice, if necessary. Already you'll be able to tell a few things about her personality. If she runs or slinks away and you can't coax her to you, she's probably going to be a shy and submissive dog who will need lots of patient training and reassurance if she's to have a normal social life. If she's at the other end of the spectrum and trounces you merrily while chewing on your clothes, biting at your hair and barking, she's likely to be a dominant, brassy dog to whom you'll need to lay down the law firmly.

Ideally, either she'll come right to you and play gently, or she'll start off timidly but grow accustomed to you in a minute or so. If she nips or mouths a little bit, don't hold it against her; that's a normal puppy behavior, and she only needs to be taught to keep her teeth to herself. But if she's obnoxiously overbearing, or if she bites hard, be wary. If she's worried about you at first, that too may be a completely normal response to this new situation. But if she's so scared that she shakes, growls or hides, she may not be the one for you. You want her to be curious and confident; she should accept your petting, scratching and cheerful talking without biting you or cowering. Watch for a wagging tail and a head held high!

This little puppy is trusting enough to hang loose without struggling or being frightened.

Pick a puppy who doesn't mind spending time in your arms!

Next, get up and walk across the room, patting your leg or clapping your hands encouragingly as you go. If she follows willingly, that's a great sign. If she follows *so* willingly that she feels the need to bite your ankles or attack your feet, that's another indication of a dominant, demanding disposition. And if she stays put or heads in the other direction, that's a sign of shyness or just plain lack of interest. You want her to be responsive and intrigued, not overbearing, scared or bored.

Now you're going to hold the puppy in three different positions that will make her feel submissive to you and establish you as an authority figure. These are exercises that closely approximate what a mother dog might do to her pup, or what an "alpha" wolf might do to a lesser pack member. They don't hurt, but they do put you temporarily in charge of the puppy's movements, and her reactions will tell you something about her willingness to accept your leadership. (If you already know that you're dealing with a puppy who's so dominant that she's aggressive, skip these and move on to another pup; you don't want to risk getting badly scratched or bitten.)

To begin, sit down and pick the puppy up as in the first photo (we suggest sitting on the floor just in case she wriggles out of your

The eyes have it! Encourage friendly eye contact with smiles and sweet talk.

hands). Hold her in front of your face, being sure to support her completely from beneath the rib cage; don't hold her by the arms or shoulders, or she'll justifiably squeal in protest! Look into her eyes and smile at her. Does she struggle, grumble and whine, or does she hang limply? A dominant puppy will fight to get free, while a submissive one won't offer any resistance at all. (If she fights you, give her a little shake and say "Hey!" or "Ah-ah!" and see whether she calms down or only grows antsier.) A happy medium is a puppy who wriggles a bit at first but then settles down and makes eye contact with you.

Then—provided the puppy is small enough—cradle her on her back in your arms as in the next photo; support her head as if she were a human baby. Look into her eyes and talk pleasantly to her. Again, note whether she kicks and screams, goes limp or something in between.

Finally, place the puppy on the floor and gently roll her onto her side, into "play-dead" position. Use one hand to stroke her head and the other to keep the rest of her body in place; don't pin her to the ground like a wrestler, but do encourage her to stay still and let you pet her. Does she struggle to get up, or does she become a rag doll under your hands? You probably know by now that what you're looking for is something in the middle: a puppy who may thrash around a bit at first but then lies quietly and accepts your authority.

By now you should have a pretty fair idea of how bossy or demure this puppy is going to be. If she's at one extreme of the spectrum or the other, she may very well be more of a challenge to train than you want, unless you're very experienced with dogs of her disposition. If she's somewhere in the middle, she'll probably turn out to be a great puppy for you: headstrong enough to be interesting and confident, but humble enough to acknowledge you as her leader after a little training. Whether you want a puppy who leans a bit to the submissive or the dominant side of the median is your choice, as long as you know what you're getting into!

Testing an Adult Dog

Now this is a more subtle process than puppy-testing. Why? For starters, most adult dogs are too big for the last three exercises outlined in the preceding section (we wouldn't want you to give yourself a hernia by trying to pick up a Rottweiler mix!). Perhaps more importantly, it's often impossible to know how an unfamiliar dog will react to your attempts to become her leader; if you catch a very self-protective dog off guard, you may be rewarded with a bite. It doesn't happen frequently, but you're wise not to take the chance, and to make your assessments in other ways instead.

Again, remember that she's going to be a little bit out of sorts when you first take her out of her cage. Give her some time to get used to you and to work out her excess energy or her initial reservations. Don't make loud noises or sudden moves; just let her bounce around for a moment and sniff and greet you, and then take her somewhere where you can really get acquainted. At no time should you grab at an unfamiliar dog; she may interpret this as a threatening gesture and respond by snapping. If you've brought your kids with you to the shelter, ask them not to touch the dog until she's gotten accustomed to you and until you know that both parties are trustworthy!

Begin just as you'd begin with a puppy: crouch down and pet her and play with her. Does she accept and enjoy your affection, or does she act suspicious of you or ignore you altogether? Does she trample and nip you, or does she avoid you? Look for something in the middle: a dog who plays and cuddles with you enthusiastically but not obnoxiously or fearfully.

Take a little walk around the room. Does she trot after you, or does she seem relieved to see you go? She should follow you happily without

Get to know each other! This Labrador mix impressed his potential adopters by bringing them three tennis balls at once.

attacking your legs or cowering from you. If you have a toy, toss it for her. Does she show interest, or does she turn up her snout at your attempt at a game?

Keep petting her, talking to her, and playing with her. If she seems at all aggressive—if she growls or snaps at you, or raises her hackles or curls her lip—move on to another dog. Unless you're an experienced dog trainer, you don't want to mess with an aggressive dog. If she doesn't appear dangerous but is nevertheless very rough or mouthy, she still may be too dominant for you.

If she slinks around and avoids looking at you, she's probably a submissive dog who will need lots and lots of positive reinforcement. Some dogs may cower or shake when you try to pet them; many people immediately interpret this as a sign that the dog has been hit or beaten, but that's not always the case. Adult dogs often shrink away from human hands simply because they've never been socialized and have never gotten used to being touched and petted. If a dog seems wary of your touch at first but begins to accept your affection after a few minutes, chances are that she'll be able to come out of her shell pretty quickly with some good training and lots of love. If she remains nervous and terrified, though, it's probably going to be a real challenge to turn her into a happy and comfortable member of society, and perhaps she's better left to someone who's had lots of experience working with undersocialized or abused dogs.

If she's lethargic and draggy, there's a good chance that poor health is to blame. Look elsewhere. You don't want to adopt a dog who may be sick.

Be on the lookout for a dog who's cheerful, responsive, and confident. But as we said in the previous section, there's plenty of leeway within those categories, depending on what kind of personality you want your dog to have.

Maybe the most important factor to consider as you evaluate a shelter dog is this: Do you enjoy her company? Do you have fun playing with her and paying attention to her, or does she leave you tired and annoyed? Often, when we meet people who are having troubles with their adopted dogs, their biggest fundamental problem seems to be that they just don't *like* their dogs very much. You don't have to adore every dog in the world any more than you have to adore every person in the world, but you certainly shouldn't adopt a dog if you're not crazy about her!

Spend as much time as you need to get to know as many dogs as you can; make more than one visit if necessary, but don't forget that a dog who catches your eye one day may be adopted by someone else or even euthanized the next, so you'll have to judge for yourself how long it's safe to wait. Take generous notes on the ones who interest you, and ask plenty of questions. Only after you've been to a number of shelters and met all the dogs, taken all the notes and asked all the questions you can stand is it time to move on to . . .

Step 5: Pick the Pup for You!

This isn't a decision that has to be made at the shelter. You might prefer to make it at home, with the help of your notes and the input of your family. Thinking logically about your canine choices is easier to do when you're not right in the midst of all the dogs in question—when you don't feel pressured for time and you're not being stared at by hopeful-looking dogs (or shelter employees!).

Maybe, by the time you've been through the first few steps of the selection process, one dog has already emerged as the clear frontrunner, and you're ready to bring her home and make her one of the family. Or maybe you've decided that none of the pups you've met so far is *the* one, and you're going to keep looking.

But if you've narrowed it down to two or three, your job now is to decide which one will be best for you, and that's a tall order. Start by going back and visiting them all again; the second time around, one may pull ahead of the pack. Go over the notes you've taken and discuss each prospect with everyone in the family. It may require a little hand-wringing or perhaps some divine inspiration, but sooner or later you'll come up with a winner.

Now, while you don't want to rush this important decision, you also don't want to take too long, or the dog you want may be gone by the time you come back. Don't forget to tell the shelter manager which dogs you think you might adopt, and find out whether they'd be willing to "hold" any of them for twenty-four or forty-eight hours. Most shelters will be reluctant to hold a dog for you if another suitable person comes and wants to adopt her, but you can ask. And *absolutely* be sure that she's not going to be euthanized within the few days after your first visit, when you might be coming back for her.

What if you really can't decide between two dogs, or you feel guilty picking one and leaving another behind? As we've said, we'd advise you against trying to adopt both at once; one new dog at a time is enough of an investment, and if you introduce two to your home simultaneously, you may be inviting some territorial battles between them to determine who got there first. Talk to the shelter people about your dilemma. They may be able to tell you objectively which dog they think would be more appropriate for you. And about that one you have to leave behind, well, perhaps you know someone else who's looking for a terrific dog and would like to take her home!

Step 6: Details, Details

The next chapter will help you know what to do and what to expect when you actually bring your new dog home from the shelter. But there are a few matters we should cover before you walk out the door with leash in hand and smile on face.

First, find out exactly what kind of medical care your dog-to-be has had. Does she still need vaccinations? If so, which ones? Has she or he been spayed or neutered? Is she on any medication? If so, for how long will she need to take it, and how should you administer it? You'll take her to a vet immediately, so be certain that you'll be allowed to bring her back if she turns out to have any serious problems.

Ask what she's been eating in the shelter, and when and how often she's been eating it. You don't necessarily have to stick to this diet and schedule, but you'll at least want to wean her from it gradually. Does she have any odd eating habits or preferences that you should know about?

You might also ask whether she has any favorite toys or activities. Does she prefer tennis balls or stuffed animals? Would she rather chase a stick or go for a jog? Does she like to sleep on a warm blanket or a cool floor? The more you know about your new dog before you take her in, the smoother her transition will be for everybody!

When you adopt your dog, you'll probably be asked to fill out some forms and sign a contract. Good shelters, as we mentioned in the last chapter, like to keep in touch with their dogs and the people who adopt them.

We probably aren't the first people to tell you this, but read your contract carefully before you put your John Hancock on it! Perhaps, as we suggested in Chapter 3, you've already looked over the contract, but if not, do it now—and when you get home, file your copy of the agreement in a safe place. Make sure you know that you'll probably have to spay or neuter your dog within a certain period of time (if it hasn't already been done), and you'll most likely have to agree to return the dog to the shelter (not give her away, sell her, or—heaven forbid—abandon her) if you're unable to keep her. Those aren't just formalities; they're important promises that you must keep.

But even more important is the unwritten contract you're signing with your new dog. You're promising to care for her and love her for as long as you're both around, in sickness and in health, for better and . . . well, you get the picture. You know by now that this is a big commitment you're making, and if you have any doubts about your ability to hold up your end of the bargain, don't put your signature on that dotted line.

But if you're confident that you've made a good choice, and you're ready and eager to do what it takes to make your new partnership work, then by all means sign your name with pride and prepare yourself for a bright and busy future with your new friend.

SUCCESS STORY #4

Lindy Gessner and Ripple
Madison, New Jersey

The dog who was to become my best friend and partner was a stray off the street when he came to the animal shelter where I work. Smelling worse than the city dump, he was an underweight, bedraggled adolescent who was frightened of everything. Yet somehow, there was a sparkle of promise in those wary eyes, and an immediate attraction between us.

I realized that his timidity was due to a total lack of socialization and experience rather than any intentional abuse. Still, abandoned and forgotten, he faced a threatening future. Even the kennel staff was skeptical of his suitability for adoption, since he appeared to be high-strung.

But despite his hatred of water and of the grooming room, he weathered the three baths we subjected him to with no more resistance than a lot of loud, anxious whining. He'd passed the "grooming" part of the shelter's temperament evaluation, so I tried some other tests. Though he was nervous and unsure of himself, he accepted being hugged, surrendered food when asked and demonstrated excellent potential for learning basic obedience tasks. As one staffer put it, "He's like a ripple— he just keeps bobbing along and coming back for more." That's how he earned the nickname "Ripple."

I knew that, as with any shelter orphan, it would take time and patience to make this adoption successful. But the connection between us was real. Decked out with a new collar and leash and high hopes for a new life together, we headed home.

My first concern was how Ripple would relate to my other animal buddies. Following the experts' advice, I introduced him to my other dog, Raja (also a shelter alumnus), on the neutral ground of a local park in order to avoid territorial aggression. I didn't need to worry. Angel that he was, Raja happily said hello, initiated a game of tag and eagerly offered to show his new friend the way home.

We established a regular routine to help Ripple adjust and feel secure, and he also came to accept his dog crate as his special place. I had seriously considered the needs of all my resident animal friends before I decided to adopt another dog, but I quickly found out that it could indeed be difficult to give each pet a fair share of attention—especially the two dogs. But exercising them was easier, since they enjoyed playing with each other, and each one learned to wait patiently (if anxiously) for his turn to be fed, groomed or trained.

I'd always wanted to teach a dog basic obedience using positive, reward-driven training methods. And Ripple proved to be a most intelligent and eager student. While I can't say that he was the outstanding star of our obedience classes, he was always in the top percentile. Unlike the other dogs in the class, Ripple was an all-American mixed breed, and some people seemed to feel an initial prejudice against us, but Ripple and I inevitably won the respect of our classmates by being a loving, seriously bonded team who thoroughly enjoyed working together.

Once Rip knew the basics, I invited Raja to join our home practice sessions. Raja, already an accomplished worker boasting a Companion Dog Excellent title, was a superb example, and Ripple learned a lot from working with him. But I never forgot that they were individuals, and I enjoyed the challenge of encouraging each of them to be his very best.

The biggest surprise I got was discovering that Ripple was terrified of children. The mere sight of a youngster, even fifty feet away, was enough to send him scurrying in panic. Although our immediate family included no children, it pained me to see him so afraid of a large sector of the population, so we made a concentrated effort to visit playgrounds, softball games, any places where children could be found. We began at a distance and gradually were able to approach closer, until the happy day when he finally accepted a treat and a petting from a little girl.

In the six years that we've shared, Ripple has mastered obedience, flyball and tracking, and has received Canine Good Citizen, Therapy Dog, and Temperament Test certificates. Each week he's my devoted partner when I teach Agility classes. He was even chosen to be a poster dog for an ad campaign encouraging people to adopt from shelters—impressive accomplishments for a dog who was considered too high-strung to be adopted! True to his name, Ripple's always bobbing along, ready for fun, and I feel most fortunate that this shelter pup "strayed" into my life.

CHAPTER 5

Bringing Your New Dog Home

Adoption day!

Finally, after all your planning and choosing, it's time to whisk your new buddy out of the shelter and into your home and heart. Her entry into the real world is going to have its ups and downs (whose doesn't?), but you can help keep things running as smoothly as possible by knowing what to expect and making some preparations ahead of time.

Before You Bring your Dog Home . . .

You've heard of "childproofing"—well, you're probably going to have to do a little "puppyproofing" to your house or apartment. It's a good idea to limit a new dog's domain to one or two rooms at the beginning, and then let her earn her freedom room by room. So decide now which parts of your house will be fair game for your pup. Kitchens are a great place to start: They usually have hard floors for easy clean-ups, and there's plenty of human activity (after all, someone's always making a trip to the refrigerator). Don't plan to leave your dog alone in a room with damageable flooring, breakable objects or chewable furniture, or in one that's seldom visited by family members.

Even if your kitchen (or whichever room you designate as your temporary canine quarters) has a door, we suggest you use a baby gate to keep your dog from escaping. It will let your dog see out and you see in, and that will save both of you some worry. Make sure you pick up everything from the floor and put any wastebaskets or recycling bins out of harm's way, and push everything on your countertops as far back as possible, since an enterprising medium-sized or large dog may figure out how to snatch food or containers if they're left within reach. If you have cabinets at doggie level, you may want to cover their corners and handles with aluminum foil to discourage chewing.

Think of your pup's safety, too: Be especially sure that all your cleaning products and other chemicals are locked away where they won't be discovered and ingested. Don't leave sharp utensils lying around, either, and remember to unplug small appliances so that your dog won't chew their cords when you're not watching.

By the time you've done all that, your kitchen may look a little like a padded cell. That's okay; once your new dog learns the rules of the house, you can put things back where they belong, but for now it's better to be safe than to risk coming home some day and finding your kitchen a shambles!

Take the same sorts of precautions in all other rooms to which your dog will have access. You'll be supervising her, of course, at least in the beginning, so you need not remove every stick of furniture and rip up every carpet just yet, but do put fragile items out of reach and cover up pieces of furniture that could be easily broken or stained. Protect your houseplants; not only may they look like tempting digging gardens to a bored dog, but some may even be poisonous. Again, don't leave exposed electrical cords plugged in, and put ashtrays well out of reach since cigarette butts can be toxic.

Now that you've fortified the castle, how about some munitions? Following is a list of supplies that your new puppy or dog will need; some of them can wait until after you've brought her home, but some—like the leash and the crate—will prove useful right from the minute you pick her up.

A crate. We'll discuss the use of the crate later in this chapter, but suffice it to say that having one and using it properly is going to save you and your dog a lot of trouble. It's useful for housebreaking, bedtime, traveling and anytime you need to confine your dog without hassle. You can buy crates at pet-supply stores and through catalogs. Whether you get the rigid plastic kind or the collapsible metal kind is up to you, but do get one that will be big enough for your dog to stand up and turn around in—but not too much bigger than that. If your dog still has some growing to do, go ahead and get a crate that will probably accommodate her when she's full-grown, and block off part of it for housebreaking purposes in the beginning (more on that later). Crates range from $50 to $200 new, but you can probably find a used one if you're persistent; check the classifieds and ask your vet or local kennels, which may even have old ones that they'll give you for free.

A leash. Your leash is going to be one of your main tools for communicating with and teaching your dog, so pick out one you like. Choose a four- or six-foot leash made of cotton, nylon or some other fabric (not chain or plastic) and of an appropriate width (a tiny toy dog doesn't need an inch-wide leash, while a Saint Bernard mix will snap a spaghetti-like leash with one lunge). Don't buy a leash with a huge snap on it, as that will get in your way when you're training. Most importantly, find a leash that's nice and soft and flexible and doesn't hurt your hands when you grasp or pull it. A fairly recent (and, as far as we're concerned, *brilliant!*) innovation in the world of doggie supplies is the retractable leash, which allows your dog to roam away from you while remaining under your control. Retractable leashes aren't cheap— they range from $15 to $35, based on their size and length—and it takes a little practice to get proficient with them, but they're well worth the investment!

Collars. She'll need two: one for training and one for wearing around the house. (If you don't know how big your dog's neck is, wait and fit her with a collar later, since a good fit is important.) The first, explained in Chapter 6 and used for training *only*, should probably be a chain or fabric slip collar—the kind often called a "choke chain," although we object to that misnomer on the grounds that a slip collar becomes a choke collar *only* if it's used improperly. A dog *can* get hurt if her slip collar gets caught on something and she pulls it tight around her neck; and that's why you'll get her another collar, one made of fabric with a buckle or safety snap, which she'll wear when she's off-duty. (If your dog is still growing, check her collar every week to make sure it's not getting too tight.)

Food and water bowls. You don't have to go out and buy these; there's nothing wrong with recycling some old cookware if you want! Just make sure they're appropriately sized, easy to clean and sturdy enough that they won't be easy to destroy (one of us has a dog who enjoys putting his head in his water bucket and flinging it across the back yard; *your* dog may come up with an even better method by which to abuse her dishes!).

Food. No sense in having a food bowl if you don't have anything to put in it. Consult your vet about what kind of food—and how much of it—your puppy or dog should eat, and introduce the new diet gradually if it's different from what your dog ate in the shelter.

Grooming tools. A comb and a brush are beauty musts for any dog! Choose a strong metal or plastic comb (an old one of yours is fine) and a brush that suits your dog's hair type. And don't forget the shampoo. A bath is going to be one of the first things on your new dog's agenda—count on it!—so buy yourself a bottle of good-quality dog shampoo (human shampoo is too harsh for dogs). You might also want to stock up on flea spray or powder if you live in a flea-prone area—especially during the summer or fall. Buy a nail clipper, too, and ask your vet to show you how to use it; by trimming your dog's toenails every two or three weeks, you can help prevent foot problems, digging and painful scratches!

A bed. Your dog will appreciate having something soft to cuddle up on, but you don't have to go buy a fancy doggie bed unless you want to; an old towel or folded-up bedspread will do just fine. (Machine washability is a plus.) Some companies make soft rectangular doggie "mats," which are a hit with humans and canines alike, since they aren't terribly expensive, they fit nicely into crates, and they're easy to roll up for traveling.

Toys. People tend to shower their pups with playthings, not realizing that sometimes less is more. Three or four really exciting toys at a time is plenty; if your dog finds herself swimming in a sea of objects, not only will she cease to appreciate them, but she may begin to think that *every* mouth-sized item in your house is her property! Choose a variety of sturdy, safe toys: hard rubber balls and knotted rope bones

are great, while small balls and flimsy rubber squeakies
lowed or shredded by large or over-enthusiastic dogs.
employee what your new dog likes to play with, and sho_
(A word of warning: Don't give her your old shoes or clothes; she may
eventually grow tired of your hand-me-downs and raid your closet
for something new and fashionable!)

A pooper scooper. You're going to be taking your dog lots of places,
and being the responsible person you are, you'll always clean up her
messes. Invest in a scoop or some other sort of waste pick-up device—
even just a supply of plastic kitchen bags—so that your dog won't be one of
the ones encouraging anti-dog sentiments in your city or neighborhood.

There's one more thing you should do just before you get your new
dog from the shelter: *Find a veterinarian* if you don't already have one
you trust, and make an appointment for your pup. We can't stress enough
how important this is. In fact, it's not a bad idea to go straight from the
shelter to the vet's office when you first get your dog. If, by some terrible chance, she has a medical problem that will make it impossible or
unwise for you to keep her, you need to find that out *now*—not after
you've spent a week or two getting attached to her. If she has some
problem that's treatable, you'll want to start taking care of it immediately. If she needs vaccinations or heartworm preventative, you can take
care of that too. And if she has any conditions that could be contagious
to other animals (or to humans, though these are rare), you'll have to
learn how to keep them from spreading. Finally, unless it's already been
done, you can schedule your dog's spaying or neutering. So ask around,
locate a competent and friendly vet, and schedule a visit.

Making the Transition . . .

You've puppy-proofed your house and filled it up with doggie goodies.
Now all you need is the dog. In your hurry to zoom to the shelter, don't
forget to put a leash in your pocket (along with a checkbook, unless
you've paid your adoption fee in advance) and a crate, if you've got
one, in the car. If you don't have a crate or some way to keep your
puppy or dog confined in the car, bring a family member or friend who
can hold her still in the back seat, since she may not be used to traveling. (We once encountered a man who made his Labrador Retriever
ride in the trunk of his car. Needless to say, that's no place for a dog!)
You might want to cover the seat with an old sheet or blanket, since
your dog may not be exactly a paragon of cleanliness just yet.

By the way, don't plan any big welcome-home celebrations; the culture shock for your dog will be less jarring if you keep things rather calm in the beginning. This isn't the time to invite the whole family over. They can wait a few days, until your dog has begun to settle into her new routine.

At the shelter, ask the employees any final questions you may have, take advantage of any handouts or other materials they offer you, and cross all your *t*'s and dot all your *i*'s. Then snap on that leash and lead your dog into her new life!

A Dog by Any Other Name

First things first: we can't keep calling this sweet creature "the new dog" forever. Maybe your dog already has a name that you like. Great! But if she's nameless, or if you hate the name she's got, you need to pick out a good one for her. (And don't let anyone tell you that it's impossible to change a dog's name—it's not.) Don't saddle her with something silly or cutesy that you might get tired of later, and don't set yourself up for a lifetime of weary jaws by giving her an overly long or tongue-twisting moniker. Pick something short and easy to say, with a nice distinctive sound so that she'll know it's all hers. Then use it; she'll figure out in no time flat that it's referring to *her*, and she'll look forward to hearing it!

And while we're on the subject, it's never too early to order some identification tags for your pup. Get two so that you have a backup in case one gets lost; you can probably find an order form at the shelter or at your vet's office. They come in plastic or metal, all different colors, and shapes ranging from circles to doggie bones to fire hydrants. But all that really matters is that your name, address and phone number appear clearly on the tag—and that you remember to get a new one if any of that information changes.

This little terrier mix is proud to wear her shiny new identification tags!

While you're waiting for your tags to be made, attach some temporary identification to your dog's collar, or write your name and phone number in permanent ink on the collar itself. It's vital that she wear some sort of ID during her first few weeks with you, since she won't yet be used to calling your place home, and she may try to wander away.

Visiting the Veterinarian

Even if your pup has already been vaccinated, wormed, and spayed or neutered, he or she still needs to go to the vet immediately. She needs to be checked for any hidden medical problems and put on heartworm preventative or any other medication she may need. And the three of you all need to get to know and trust each other *now*, rather than waiting until an emergency arises.

Bring a sample of your dog's stool with you on your first visit, and bring any medical records the shelter has given you. You can take your dog on her leash and collar unless she's a little puppy, in which case a small crate or pet carrier is best. The vet's office can be a scary place to some dogs and an incredibly exciting place to others, so be prepared either to comfort her or to keep her under tight control. Don't let her come into contact with any of the other animals in the waiting room; you don't want any germs to be passed around.

Tell the vet when and where you adopted your dog, and share with him or her whatever you know about her medical history—in particular, what vaccinations she's had. And don't be afraid to ask questions; here are a few to keep in mind:

1. What vaccinations does she still need, and when?

2. What and how much should I feed her?

3. If she needs pills, how often should I administer them, and can you show me how to give them to her?

4. If she needs heartworm preventative, how should I administer it? (Heartworm is a mosquito-transmitted parasite that's difficult and expensive to treat but easy to prevent.)

5. How should I clip her nails?

6. If she's not already spayed or he's not neutered, when should it be done? (See Chapter 7 for a full discussion of spaying and neutering.)

7. When should we come back for her next checkup?

It's a good idea to pick one vet and stick with him or her for the life of your dog. But if you don't feel comfortable with your vet after this initial visit—if you feel that he or she was too brusque with your dog or didn't answer your questions satisfactorily—now is the time to find another one. Otherwise, make the most of your relationship, and don't hesitate to ask for your vet's help and advice throughout your life with your adopted dog.

The First Day and Night

When you get home, take a few minutes to show your puppy or dog around the yard, but don't introduce her to the neighbor's dogs just yet unless your vet has given you permission to do so. Then bring her inside and let the family get to know her—slowly. Don't crowd around her all at once and make lots of noise, or she'll think she's been adopted by the Addams Family and will begin plotting her escape (just kidding).

Show her the room where she'll be spending most of her time, and point out her food and water bowls, her toys and her crate. The next place you'll probably want to take her is the bathtub. Give her a good brushing and scrubbing and a flea bath if necessary. You can also carefully wipe out the insides of her ears with alcohol-soaked cotton balls (one for each ear—don't double up, or you'll put the nasty stuff from one ear right into the other!). You'll be amazed at how much better she'll look and feel after a good cleaning-up, and it's smart to get her into the habit of being "beautified," since you'll be bathing and brushing her regularly from now on.

If she hasn't eaten recently, she may want a small meal. Don't give her too much food, since traveling and being in a new environment may have upset her stomach, and don't be surprised if she's not yet in the mood to chow down. (You don't all have to watch her eat, either; that may make her even more nervous than she probably already is, and anyway, you're not going to want her staring at you when it's *your* dinnertime.) It's not uncommon for a new dog to have some strange eating habits or a bit of diarrhea during her first day or so with you, but if problems persist, consult your vet.

Don't forget to take her out to relieve herself every now and then. Again, travel and nervousness may make her less able than usual to control herself, and you surely don't want her to get into the habit of answering nature's calls in your house.

Where should she sleep? How about in her crate by your bed? The next section will discuss how to get your dog used to crating. It's not much trouble to move the crate from the kitchen to the bedroom at night, and that way she'll be close to you without being able to trample you or (if she's an insomniac) wander around and wreak havoc on your room. She'll like the feeling of being in your presence, even when she's asleep, and you'll probably like her company too.

That said, it's only fair for us to confess that we've both been known to let our dogs sleep on, and even *in,* our beds. (Really, there's nothing better for keeping your feet warm in the winter.) So we'd hardly condemn you for doing the same, but we strongly suggest that you not let her share your bed right at the beginning; in dog language, that's like an acknowledgment that she is your equal in the family "pack," and it may encourage her to challenge your authority in other ways. Start with her in the crate beside you, and later she can graduate to the bed *if:*

1. She's completely housebroken and trustworthy;

2. She's not a dominant type who might eventually decide that the bed belongs to her (we've met a little Lhasa Apso who once commandeered a twin bed and threatened to attack anyone who came near it);

3. She knows that it's your bed, not hers, and she must evacuate it on command; and

4. You don't mind having a bit of fur on your comforter and a big lug of a dog taking more than her share of covers.

The real trick during your first few days with your new adopted puppy or dog will be managing to supervise her and keep her company without overwhelming her with excess attention. If you leave her alone too much, she'll get into mischief or become lonely and confused. But if you try to follow her around constantly, you'll both be exhausted, and she won't learn to how to get along on her own.

So what's the solution? We suggest that you try the *"umbilical cord"* *method* endorsed by the late and indisputably great dog trainer and dog writer Job Michael Evans. Just snap a leash on your dog and attach the other end of it to your belt loop, and let your pup trail you around the house for a while. (If she decides to chew on her leash, spray or rub a little lemon juice or vinegar on it.) That lets you keep an eye on her

Sam doesn't mind being umbilical-corded to Bill, especially when it means she gets free concerts.

without having to trail her like a private eye; it means that she has the freedom to walk around, but *you're* calling the shots and determining where to go. This isn't just a practical plan; it will also help establish some good patterns. By spending time in your presence and going where you go, she's going to start learning that you're her friend, protector and leader—not someone for her either to fear or to boss around. She'll bond with you and learn your ways quickly. And she'll get used to being on a leash; in the next chapter we'll talk about teaching your dog to walk with you on her leash, using the command "Let's go!" You'll find that umbilical-cording will help make that process a smooth one and vice versa.

Perhaps you've gleaned by now that we think supervision really is one of the keys to having a responsible, happy and well-behaved dog! If you can spend a few hours a day leashed to your dog during her first week, she'll learn fairly quickly how to conduct herself appropriately in the house. After all, she can't do much wrong when you're there to correct her. But what should you do when you can't be physically attached to her? That's when the crate becomes important.

Introducing the Crate

We humans value our freedom at all costs, and that leads some people to gasp in horror at the notion of crating a dog. A few years ago, in fact, a nationally syndicated advice columnist caused a furor by printing a letter from a veterinarian advocating crating for dogs who destroyed property in their houses. The vet's advice was right on target, but readers from around the nation bombarded the poor columnist with indignant and unpleasant letters demanding how anyone could be so cruel. We sometimes hear similar attitudes (usually put less nastily, thank goodness!) from our adopters and obedience-class students, and we respond with the question, "Would you think a parent was cruel for keeping a baby in a playpen for a few hours a day, rather than letting him crawl unsupervised around the house, where he could get hurt or break something?"

It's a rare client who can honestly answer "yes" to that question. And remember that dogs are den animals who like to have cozy, safe spaces to call their own. A crate is cruel *only* if it's physically uncomfortable, or if a dog is left in it too often or for too long at a stretch. And the crate is never to be used or thought of as a punishment, though you can certainly let your dog unwind in it if she gets a little hyper or needs some "time out."

Of course, the crate shouldn't become a cop-out either. The idea isn't to shut your pup in her crate and leave her there every time she gets in your way or on your nerves. If you find yourself tempted to do that too often, that probably means that your dog needs more training in order to make her easier to live with, or that you need to find a little more time to spend with her. So use the crate judiciously. Think of it not as a prison, but as a playpen or a den—and as a huge help to you in housebreaking and supervising—and don't waste time feeling guilty.

Introduce your dog to her crate slowly, using a toy or a treat and lots of soothing speech to lure her in. (Don't apologize to her for incarcerating her; act as though the crate is the most wonderful place in the world to be, and you'd be in there with her if you thought you could both fit.) You can attach a phrase to this action—"go in your crate," maybe, or "kennel up"—so that she'll eventually learn to head to her den on command. For now, keep the crate fairly bare—no bedding necessary, since she may chew it or relieve herself on it. Some shelter dogs will be used to being crated, thanks to the time they've spent

You *and* your dog will benefit from a crate, which is only cruel if it's too small or if your dog is kept in it too often.

in cages, while others may react unhappily or even frantically to being confined. If your dog is of the latter persuasion, take it slowly. Don't make matters worse by forcing her into the crate or yelling at her for her hesitation. If you're patient and encouraging, chances are excellent that you'll be able to persuade her to give the crate a try, even if only for a few seconds at first.

Don't immediately expect your dog to stay alone in a crate for hours at a time, especially if she's not yet housebroken. She should *never* be crated for more than four or five hours without a chance to stretch her legs, and you'll have to work up to that. For now, there's nothing wrong with using a little bribery (toys or occasional treats) to keep your dog happy in her crate, as long as you don't overdo it, and as long as you're careful not to treat her at the wrong times. In other words, *don't* give her a biscuit in an attempt to calm her down when she's barking or scrabbling around in her crate, or she'll learn that all she has to do to get a snack is make a fuss! Instead, wait until she's being quiet and pleasant to slip her a bite.

If she does get noisy and disruptive in her crate, give her a minute or two to settle down; if she persists, then whack the top of the crate (but not the dog, please!) loudly with a magazine or some other whackable item. You need not say a word. In fact, it's probably better if you don't, since her whole aim in making a stink is to get your attention, and you don't want to reward her theatrics. A loud smack on the crate, on the other hand, is a "bolt-from-the-blue" correction that will catch her by surprise and, after a few repetitions, convince her that there are better ways to pass time in a crate.

Use that same patented whack during the night if your pup grows restless while you're trying to sleep. Have her crate near to your side, and keep a magazine handy so that you can reach over and slap the crate without needing to turn on the light or say anything. (One exception, which we'll discuss further in the next section: If there's any chance that she legitimately needs to go outside, honor that request at least once, but if it becomes clear to you that it's a false alarm, re-commence whacking.)

Your dog should be in her crate any time you can't watch her. And that really means *watch* her; if you can't keep at least one eye and one ear on her, it doesn't count as supervision, and either you need to direct a bit more attention to her or she needs to go into her crate. Remember, a speedy dog can deforest your flower pots or convert your hassock into a toilet in about five seconds (less if she's an experienced criminal), so for your own sake you mustn't leave her unattended even for a moment during these first crucial days. The more vigilant you are now, the more trustworthy she'll be later.

When your dog begins to be trustworthy around the house in your presence (that is, when you no longer feel that you're always dropping what you're doing to go correct her for her mischief!), she can begin to earn her freedom little by little. Don't simply leave her out of her crate one day while you leave the house for hours on end; start by letting her wander unsupervised in one or two rooms while you're in the house, and check on her every few minutes to make sure she's not pulling any stunts in your absence. Gradually increase the number of rooms to which she has access until you're confident that she can be trusted out of your eyesight and earshot.

The next step is letting her win her freedom when you're not home. You may decide that you simply don't want her roaming the house when you're not there, and that's okay; you can designate one specific room where she'll remain when the house is empty, or she can stay in her crate if she won't be left alone for more than a few hours. But if you'd like to be able to leave her to her own devices, go slowly. Set her free to explore one or two rooms some day when you run out to do a quick errand, and gradually—very gradually—increase the number of rooms available to her and the length of time she's alone.

Even if she's a model house dog in your absence, she may at some point (especially during adolescence, when the urge to chew and rebel is strongest) hit a mischievous streak. If your previously perfect pup suddenly becomes a miscreant, perhaps she's had too much freedom too soon and needs to be crated and supervised again. (She's probably also bored and could use some more exercise; Chapters 6 and 7 offer some ideas.)

A word of caution: Beware of hysterical hellos and goodbyes when you're teaching your dog to stay home by herself. An overemotional departure will clue her in that something is amiss, and she may react by becoming worried and destructive. Make your comings and goings as matter-of-fact as possible, and she won't have to fret that you're leaving her for good.

Using the Crate for Housebreaking

Your dog's den instincts are going to be a big help to you as you housebreak her. Bear in mind that dogs, unlike teenagers, have a strong tendency to keep their immediate living spaces neat and clean. That means

Sam isn't quite convinced that the great outdoors really is the best bathroom for her. Jessica will keep sweet-talking her until she gets the idea.

that your dog is unlikely to use her crate/den as a restroom, unless the crate's too large, in which case she may relieve herself in one corner and retreat to the opposite corner, thinking she's kept her area clean. Unfortunately for you, dogs' dens are usually pretty small and cozy, which means that while your pup may not relieve herself in her crate, she probably won't feel any natural compunction about doing so in your living room. So your job during the housebreaking process will be to convince her that your whole house or apartment is her extended den and is thus not to be used as a Johnny-on-the-spot.

By most estimates, housebreaking problems are the number-one reason that people give their dogs up for adoption. That's very sad, because—contrary to popular belief—housebreaking really doesn't have to be all that difficult! And you can make the job even easier on yourself if, as you venture into the exciting world of potty-training, you let these four simple commandments guide you:

Rule #1: The key to housebreaking is scheduling. You're going to have to establish a firm routine and stick to it until your dog gets the hang of housebreaking. If she knows when to expect to be taken outside, she soon won't mind waiting until her next scheduled outing. But if she never knows when or whether she's going to get to go out, she may decide it's not worth her while to control herself.

Rule #2: What goes in must come out. In other words, if your dog is nibbling and sipping all day long, she's going to need to go to the bathroom all day long. So it's important that you schedule her food intake and keep snacks to a minimum, and you can even schedule her water intake at the beginning. Of course, if it's very hot or if your dog is getting lots of exercise, then she needs to have fresh water available to her all day long. But otherwise, you can give her periodic drinks throughout the day so that you'll know when she'll need to go out—probably about ten to thirty minutes after drinking or eating.

Rule #3: In housebreaking as in stand-up comedy, timing is everything. Your dog is going to have accidents—count on it—and the only way you're going to teach her right from wrong is to catch her in the act and correct her. Correcting her after the fact won't do a bit of good, because she won't know what she did or why you're upset with her. And that's why it's so important—stop us if you've heard this before—that you supervise her scrupulously during these early days.

Rule #4: Cleanliness counts. Dogs will almost always return to spots that they've soiled before. So if your dog has one accident on the couch, she's likely to have another, unless you thoroughly disinfect and deodorize the area. And remember, her nose is a lot more sensitive than yours, so you're going to have to do some heavy-duty scrubbing to make sure that no traces remain. Your best bet is to use one of the commercial sprays or solutions designed for this very task.

Until your pup is reliable (and remember, if she's under about six months old, she won't even have full physical control of herself yet), she's not going to be allowed to spend time around the house unless you can watch her and unless she's recently been outside to relieve herself. So you'll take her out first thing in the morning, and then she can have some supervised playtime. If she eats a morning meal, you'll take her out after that. And so on at regular intervals throughout the day. She'll probably need to go out four or five times, and more if she's a puppy. Basically, she earns her freedom in the house by doing her business outside. By this plan, she's not so likely to have accidents in the house, and even if she does, you'll be there to set her straight.

When you take your pup outside, really *take* her outside; don't just *put* her outside. If you simply turn her loose into your fenced yard for ten minutes, chances are that she'll spend them waiting and worrying about whether she's going to get to come back in rather than doing her duty, and then when she *does* come back in, she may be so excited that she'll have an accident on the floor. (People often say to us, "My dog always goes outside and then comes back in and looks straight at me and goes on the floor. Is she being spiteful?" Nah—this is usually just a result of the scenario just described.) Even if you put her outside and she does just what she's supposed to do, it's important for you to be there to tell her what a good girl she is to go in the proper place.

So take her out on her leash and use a phrase like "Do your thing" or "Hurry up" to encourage her to go; eventually, she'll recognize that phrase and will be able to go on command. When she relieves herself, make a big fuss—never mind those funny looks from your neighbors—and let her know that she is the very best dog in the whole world. Use the same door for all your trips so that she'll eventually learn to wait by it when she needs to go out.

By the way, don't necessarily whisk her back indoors immediately after she's done her business. If you do, she may learn that going to the bathroom does little more than cut short her outdoor playtime. So let her do what she needs to do, and *then* spend a few minutes walking her and playing with her before you head back inside.

If you take her outside and she doesn't do anything after a reasonable amount of time, bring her back in and put her in her crate for a while, and then try again. Remember, the freedom to roam the house (or selected rooms thereof) is always a direct result of doing her duty outdoors.

What happens if your dog has—gulp—an accident indoors? Well, first of all, if you don't catch her *as* it's happening, you *cannot* correct her for it. Period. Dogs have incredibly short short-term memories, and even though it may take *you* a long time to forget that she stained your favorite throw rug, it'll be only a matter of seconds before she's erased the incident from her mind. The only thing you can do if you discover a mishap after the fact is to clean it up and scold yourself for not watching her more carefully. *Never* rub a dog's nose in her mess, and *never* hit a dog for having an accident. That will efficiently teach her to fear and disrespect you, and it'll probably make her housebreaking problems even worse.

Don't fool yourself into thinking that your dog looks "guilty" for her crime if you correct her for an earlier mistake. Even if she looks sad and contrite, she's not feeling repentant; she's probably just reacting to your displeasure and wondering what she possibly could have done to deserve it. That goes for all sorts of doggie no-no's, not just house-breaking mistakes: both of us, for example, have multiple dogs, and when we scold one of them, the others who have done nothing wrong invariably look just as penitent as the guilty party. Dogs learn not to do bad things because we teach them that their actions have immediate consequences, not because their inner moral sense tells them that soiling the furniture is inherently wrong!

If you do catch her *in flagrante*, go straight to her and say "Uh-uh! We don't do that in here" or something equally indignant. Take her by the collar (or leash, if you are still umbilical-corded to her) and lead her outside, praising her lavishly if she finishes the job there. Then park her in her crate for a few minutes while you clean up and cool off.

Like all dog training, housebreaking depends on consistency. The more conscientious you are about correcting your dog *every* time she goes indoors, praising her *every* time she goes outdoors, and taking her out *every* time you know she needs to go, the faster she'll become house-broken and the fewer slip-ups she'll have. So design a schedule by which you, your dog, and everyone else in your family will abide until your new pup is housebroken. (By the way, remember that weekdays and weekends are no different to a dog's inner workings, so if you're taking her outside at 7 A.M. Monday through Friday, you're going to have to do the same on Saturday and Sunday, at least for now.) Write down your schedule and post it on your refrigerator, and remind all humans in the household that following it religiously is in everyone's best interests!

If everyone complies, you'll notice fairly soon that she'll start letting you know when she needs to go out. She may bark or whine to tell you that it's that time, or she may go and stand by the door. Always respond to her signals as promptly as you can, and let her know what a good pup she is to be so communicative. If you get outside and discover that it was a false alarm, don't be too hard on her (after all, you don't want to teach her not to give you notice); just bite your tongue, keep quiet, and bring her back inside.

Some dogs seem to take to housebreaking almost immediately; others don't catch on quite so quickly, and that may be true of your adopted dog, especially if she got accustomed to making messes in her cage while she was at the shelter. So give her time. But if, after a few weeks, you're really not seeing any improvement, the first thing to do is to take your dog to the vet and have her checked for any kind of parasite or infection that could be impairing her control. Then reassess your own habits: Are you (and everyone in the household) being faithful to your dog's schedule? And is that schedule a fair one, or does it make supercanine demands on her system? Are you really letting her know in the right ways that it's good to relieve herself outside and bad to relieve herself inside?

One common problem is that of the dog who piddles on the floor during playtime or when greeted. If your dog is one of these "leaky" types, *don't* treat this as a housebreaking problem. If you correct a dog who's relieving herself out of excitement or submissiveness (and that's usually the case, especially with a dog who leaves a puddle when you pet her), she'll probably just go more. Instead, try to avoid situations that are likely to set her off: discourage rowdy play, especially if she's just eaten or had a drink, and ask your family members and visitors to crouch down and act calm and quiet when they greet her. As she becomes more comfortable with your company and the company of your family and friends, she'll understand that she doesn't need to jump out of her skin in excitement or fear in your presence. And—since this problem is especially common in young pups—she'll gain better muscle control over her functions as time goes on.

Above all, be patient, and take things slowly. Just because she lets you know once that she needs to go out, that doesn't mean that you should immediately give her full run of the house. Just because she has a little setback, that doesn't mean that all your efforts have been for nothing. Housebreaking always has its ups and downs, but if you're fair and consistent, you'll prevail!

Introducing New Dogs and Old

If there's another dog already living in your home, you'll have some introductions to make. You can help avoid jealousy by making sure that each pup has her own dishes, her own toys, and her own bed, and that you don't give them rawhides or other chews (prime objects of contention) during their first days together. In time they may well learn to share their possessions, but for now it's best not to encourage them to fight over their goodies. And be absolutely certain that you don't neglect your old dog in favor of your new dog during these first few weeks. You'll be spending a lot of time with the new one, of course, so make sure the old one gets some extra walking and petting as well;

otherwise, she may be tempted to devise her own ways of getting your attention, and you may not like her tactics!

Keep both dogs on leashes when they first meet, just in case you need to separate them. It's often a good idea to let your dogs get acquainted on neutral ground, especially if you know that one or both may tend to be overly territorial. You might take them to a park or a neighbor's yard and let them sniff each other and play together for a while; that may help your old dog feel like she's bringing a friend home rather than letting a stranger into her house!

You need not turn them both loose in your house immediately;

Puppy Anton wonders how long it will be before he's as big and strong as his new friend, Barney.

for example, you can put the new pup in her crate while the elder statesdog is free in the kitchen. That will allow them to get used to each other's presence without having to be in physical contact. Don't leave them alone together until you're positive that they'll behave themselves; unless you can be certain that they won't fight, they need to be crated or in separate rooms. (If you leave them to their own devices, you also run the risk that they'll take their new friendship overboard and become partners in crime; we've seen our own dogs team up to reach countertops or open toilet lids that they couldn't manage alone!) *Do* give them plenty of supervised playtime together; it's important that they have a chance to become buddies, but you need to be with them and be ready to step in if any kind of disagreement erupts between them. (More on how to discourage fighting in Chapter 6.)

Stress: It Isn't Just for Humans Anymore!

Bringing a new family member home, though it's a wonderful experience, also comes with its share of that all-purpose nineties buzzword: stress! You're already learning the ways in which adoption is stressful

Walt and Sam agree that the best cure for the new-dog blues is a little snuggling.

on *you,* but what about its effects on your dog? This is going to be a strange time for her too, as she gets used to living in a new place with new people and new rules.

What do you do when you're "stressed out?" Bite your fingernails? Grind your teeth? Eat chocolate? We all have nervous habits—usually at least moderately self-destructive or annoying!—to which we resort when we're feeling anxious, and dogs are no different. Your dog may have or develop a few habits that will drive you crazy, and you'll have to teach her to keep her stress and its manifestations in check. Chapter 6 lists a few common annoyances and their remedies. Be firm in enforcing your rules, but do try to remember that she's not "being bad" out of insolence or ingratitude. And keep in mind that it's tough for anyone, human or canine, to kick a bad habit!

Remember, too, that exercise and entertainment are two great ways to relieve stress and get to know your new dog better. Chapter 7 suggests some activities that you and your pup can enjoy together. And be sure you spend plenty of time petting and talking to your new dog: your touch and your voice are going to be two of the most important influences and comforts in her life, and she's going to crave lots and lots of affection and communication as she grows into her new role as your special dog.

The first week or two are going to tire out your body and your mind—no doubt about that. But if you're firm, fair, and loving, you'll find that there are more than enough good times to counteract the trying ones!

SUCCESS STORY #5

Cyndy, Jim, Matt and Chris Monjat and Andy
Avon Lake, Ohio

Andy came to us about four years after our first dog, Rufus, died. Rufus had been a wonderful companion for thirteen years, and I was hesitant to take on the responsibility of another dog—especially a puppy who would need housebreaking, obedience training and all the usual needs of a pet. I didn't want to add those jobs to the job of raising two young boys, since I knew most of the chores of dog-raising would fall into my lap.

But my husband, Jim, was beginning to get anxious to have a dog for the boys to grow up with. We live in a wooded area where we knew it would be fun for the children to walk and play with a dog; our yard was custom-made for kids and pets. So Jim started checking all the local papers for ads for dogs who needed good homes. He came upon several possibilities, but none of them sounded quite right for us.

One day an ad for the OASIS Animal Shelter caught his eye. He quietly went to the shelter that morning to see one of the advertised dogs, and he came back in the afternoon with a look about him that I'd never seen before—kind of a cross between someone in love and a father with a newborn baby. He told me that he'd walked through the shelter and come face to face with a pair of big brown eyes, and that he and this dog had "bonded" immediately. The pup, whose name was Andy, had been left one morning tied to the shelter fence.

I agreed to go and meet Andy the next morning, although I was still uncertain. Jim and the shelter director, Shari, introduced me to Andy, a Collie-Shepherd mix about a year and a half old. He struck me as a nice dog right away, and my barriers started to break down, slowly. Andy had obviously had some in-house obedience training already, as he wasn't too wild and he listened fairly well, but his most outstanding feature was his soft, gentle, and friendly nature.

We made our third visit to the shelter that evening with our sons, Matt and Chris, with the idea that we would give it some more thought if they liked him. Who was I kidding? The boys walked Andy around the shelter yard, patted him, hugged him—and with my slightly nervous consent, we told told Shari we'd take him. After the paperwork was done, we loaded boys and dog into the van, and Andy was a pleasure even on that first ride home. We took him for a check-up within a couple days, and the vet was very excited for us and confirmed that Andy was a healthy animal with a friendly, sweet disposition.

At first, Andy was afraid to venture into any areas of the house except the kitchen, but as time went on, he became comfortable all around. Eventually, he found his favorite place to sit: on Jim's lap on our family-room couch, acting as if he were a ten-pound puppy instead of the sixty-pound dog he is! We took Andy to obedience school, where he won a prize for doing the longest sit-stay.

So we've all settled into family life with our new friend, who is truly a wonderful companion and a loving, *usually* obedient pet. He loves to ride with us in the car, walk with us in the woods, and rest or play with us in the yard or the house.

A year ago, our lives took a new twist when a small grey cat wandered into our yard and decided to make us her family. I was definitely skeptical about another new addition, but her gentle persistence soon made her a family member. Andy wasn't thrilled with the cat, since she robbed him of some of his attention, but slowly he learned to tolerate her, and now they even play together and try to outdo each other for our benefit.

We're all grateful that we found Andy at the animal shelter. He is an enormous blessing to all of us in many ways: he's friendly and loving, yet he is full of life and can be boisterous, too. He barks to warn us of strangers in the yard, but he's never troublesome to our friends or visitors. We really found a gem of a pet who enhances our lives every day, and we're thankful for the love and joy he brings us in return for the the simple happiness and warm home we provide for him.

CHAPTER 6

The Educated Canine

Ralph Waldo Emerson—a pretty smart guy—once said, "The secret of education is respecting the pupil." We hope you'll keep this bit of wisdom in mind as you educate your dog.

And we do mean *educate*. When most people think of dog training, they think of it as a short-term commitment: eight or ten weeks of night school designed to teach your dog to obey you. We think there's much more to it than that. Obedience class is just one important part of the lifelong process of teaching your dog what she needs to know to live in your world. Educating your dog means communicating with her: helping her understand and respond to your words and actions, and learning to respond to *her* signals. Sure, you could just drill a few commands into her brain and call her trained. But you'll both be much happier if you take the time to become familiar with each other's ways of thinking and to learn to work as a team. You'll be amazed at how much you can discover, and how much fun you can have along the way.

Educating your dog is also the best—*only*—way to get rid of whatever behavior problems she may bring with her from the shelter or develop after she moves in with you. This chapter will help you address directly some of the most common doggie discrepancies, and you'll probably find that enrolling your dog in an obedience class and training her daily will ease her errant tendencies indirectly, too, by giving her a more appropriate outlet for her physical and mental energies.

By the way, dogs of all ages can and must be trained. Puppies are ripe to be taught; don't let your little darling get away with mischief when she's young and cute, or you'll have a difficult and bad-habit-ridden dog on your hands a few months down the line. Adolescent dogs (those between six months and several years of age—the age bracket into which the majority of shelter dogs fall) are full of spit and vinegar

What's Tyler thinking behind that wrinkled brow?

and teenage energy, for better or for worse, so your young-adult dog will need and enjoy education—even if she's been trained as a puppy—since adolescence tends to bring with it some perversity and problems! And canine senior citizens are educable too, despite the tired saying about old dogs and new tricks, and they often benefit greatly from the exercise and stimulation training provides.

If you're still not convinced that education is the way to go, consider this: Dogs are *always* learning. They're forever picking up new habits, or discovering new ways to get treats or attention. So it's to your advantage to make sure that your dog learns what you want her to learn. The more time and intellect she's using on her obedience lessons, the less she'll have left over to figure out how to eat from the cookie jar or devour a good novel from your bookshelves.

"Training has given me back my dog!" a woman told us once of her West Highland White Terrier, who had been doing a Tasmanian devil act in her household before she took him to school. "It's like he's a whole new dog—one I can really enjoy!" Things can turn out just that happily for you and *your* little devil, too. So, without wasting any time, let's begin by taking at least a glance into the depths of your dog's mind.

Dog Psychology 101: An Introduction to Canine Cogitation

What do you need to know in order to train your dog? Well, the standard answer is "more than the dog," and that's a good start, but perhaps more importantly, you need to know how she thinks and learns. First of all, remember that your dog is a pack animal at heart, and your family has just become her new pack. Chances are, she's wondering whether she's expected to be the leader of this pack or one of the followers. Your job is to teach her that *you* are her leader, and a wise, just, kind leader at that. Therefore, any time when you're not feeling particularly wise, just, or kind is not the time to be training your dog.

There are two major ways in which dogs do their learning, and good dog teachers always keep both of them in the forefronts of their minds.

Repetition. Think back: How did you study for vocabulary tests when you were in grade school? Unless you had a photographic memory, reading the words and definitions only once probably didn't do the trick. So you repeated them to yourself until they were permanently inscribed into your memory, right? Your dog will need the same kind of repetition in order to remember the words and meanings you want her to know. It's a rare dog who picks up a command immediately; you can expect to remove your dog from your lounge chair or show her how to lie down many, many times before she'll reliably stay out of your seat or respond to your "down" command.

Seeking pleasure and avoiding displeasure. Quite simply, your dog is going to try very hard to do the things that are going to earn her a reward, and *not* to do the things that are going to earn her a correction. Sound obvious? It is, but you'd be surprised at how often we send mixed messages to our dogs! Here's an example: Have you ever walked down the street and encountered a dog who lunged or growled at you from the end of her leash? If so, then you know that the most common reaction from the person at the other end of the leash is to pet and soothe and sweet-talk the dog. Now that's a classic crossed-up signal, since it rewards the dog for her antisocial behavior; a more appropriate response would be a good sharp vocal and physical correction (more on those to come). We're all guilty of that kind of hypocrisy now and then, but it's important not to make it a habit, or you'll have an awfully confused dog to show for it!

Educating your dog means becoming an authority figure to her and earning her respect and allegiance as you teach what she needs to

An educated dog like Leon can be an out-and-about dog.

know. Before you dive right into her lessons, stop and think about your own education. Think about the teachers you loved and the teachers you hated. Chances are, the ones you adored and respected were the fair, calm ones who made you enjoy what you were learning, and the ones you loathed were the short-tempered, arbitrary ones who drilled you on your lessons without ever cracking a smile. Don't forget them as you educate your dog, because great teachers of kids and great teachers of canines have a whole lot in common. So in order to be a successful dog teacher, there are a couple of qualities you need to have and use liberally:

Persistence. Dog education takes time. If some videotape or book tells you that you can have a perfectly trained dog after one or two weeks, don't believe it! First of all, as we've said, dog training isn't something you can do once and then forget: Even if your dog *can* learn everything she needs to know in a week, she's not going to retain much of it if you don't keep practicing with her. Expect that your new pup will need several weeks to understand the rules of your house and the new words you'll teach her. Dogs learn at very different rates, and by the way, slower doesn't necessarily mean *dumber.*

Sometimes the brightest dogs are also the most stubborn, so keep the faith and know that *every* dog, no matter how resistant, can be educated. As you educate your dog, don't compare her to your friends' dogs or the dogs you see on TV; compare her to *herself* when you first adopted her, and be proud of the progress she's made.

Patience. Closely related to persistence is this indispensible virtue, which you'll need aplenty. Just about the worst thing you can do to your canine student is to get frustrated and yell at, hit or give up on her. There will be times when you're not going to like her very much: When she chews up your best mittens or wakes you up three nights in a row with her barking or *still* won't sit on command after approximately ten thousand repetitions. But don't get mad; if you lose your temper, she's just going to become confused and lose respect for you, and you'll probably feel guilty later on top of it. Instead of throwing a fit, simply correct her for her mishap like the calm, authoritative leader you are. Then shut yourself in the bedroom and punch a pillow.

Consistency. It's absolutely crucial that you establish rules and stick to them. Dogs have trouble with the concept of "sometimes," so if climbing on the couch is acceptable on certain days of the week, it had better be okay *all* the time. And if you allow her to beg at the table most evenings, then you can't discipline her for doing it when you have dinner guests. Decide what you're going to permit and what you're going to forbid, and then praise her every time she's good and correct her every time she errs. It's as simple as that. If you're consistent in your teachings, your dog will respect you for your fairness, and she'll learn her lessons far more quickly than if you confuse her with a lot of grey areas.

A good attitude. Nope, smiles and positive thinking alone won't educate your dog, but they'll sure make the process a lot more enjoyable for both of you. Any obedience instructor will tell you that the student *least* likely to succeed is the one who announces on the first night of class that "this is my dog's last chance because she's driving me crazy and if this doesn't work she's going to the pound," and close behind is the one who decides that "my dog is probably too [pick one] stupid/stubborn/old/incorrigible/set in her ways to learn anything." Dogs know a self-fulfilling prophecy when they hear one. Don't jinx yourself before you even begin. Keep your outlook happy and your confidence high, and your dog will likely do the same.

By the way, there are still a few people who may try to tell you that dog training is unkind. Hogwash! Schooling is the kindest thing you can do for your new friend, and you're not going to use any methods that will be painful or unfair to her. Just remind yourself (and anyone else who needs to be reminded) that educating a dog is no more "cruel" than educating a child, and don't waste your time feeling guilty or apologetic. In fact, give yourself a pat on the head instead.

Tools of the Trade

"So," you may be thinking, "when do we start learning?" Well, you know by now that we believe in applying lots of planning, patience, and forethought to every stage of the dog adoption process, and this one's no

This is how the slip collar MUST look when it's on your dog: The end that passes through the ring and attaches to the leash comes from around the left side of the dog's head.

different! Besides an understanding of how your dog thinks and learns, the other thing you'll need for your schooling is the proper equipment, most of which you probably already have.

A leash. Your four- or six-foot leash (cotton, nylon or other fabric) will be fine for training. When you go to obedience school, you'll probably want to add to your arsenal a fifteen- to twenty-five-foot "long line," which you'll use to teach your dog to respond to you from a distance.

A training collar. For most dogs, a chain slip collar—a length of chain with a metal ring at each end, often unfairly called a "choke chain"—will do the trick. Your dog will wear this collar *only* during training sessions and when you're trying to catch her in the act of misbehaving; she should never, ever wear it when she's out of your sight, since it could get caught on something and tighten around her neck. We've known dogs who died because they were left unsupervised in their training collars, and we'd never want that to happen to yours. The training collar forms a loop and fits over your dog's head; when you face your dog, the collar should look like a P—not a Q—as it slips over her head. (Look at the photo so that you'll know it should look on your dog, since most people aren't aware that there's only one correct way.) The following sections will teach you how to use the slip collar properly without hurting your dog; don't *ever* yank hard on a slip collar or allow one to remain tight around your dog's neck, or she could be seriously injured.

If you're working with a young puppy or a very timid dog, you probably won't need the extra oomph of a chain slip collar just yet. You can use her plain old buckle collar for her early lessons. Other newer training devices, like nylon harnesses or halters, are gentler and less prone to misuse and overuse than chain slip collars and can be perfect for some dogs, but you'll probably want to wait until you're enrolled in obedience school and under the guidance of an instructor.

Don't mess around with prong collars or other fancy training collars except under the supervision of a knowledgeable dog trainer. Though they unfortunately look rather nasty, prong collars are extraordinarily effective and humane training tools when used judiciously, but they're definitely not for every dog. So if other training devices aren't doing the trick and your instructor suggests that you use a prong collar, by all means take his or her advice, but don't go it alone.

A spray bottle and/or a shake can. We'll suggest that you use these handy gadgets to discourage a number of annoying canine habits. Keep a plain plastic spray bottle (or a water gun, for some real fun) filled with water handy, and practice aiming and shooting at your dog's mouth. If your dog isn't bothered by blasts of water, try mixing in some lemon juice; if your dog enjoys even *that* (and we have at least a couple who do), visit your pet-supply store and buy a bottle of a nasty-tasting solution called bitter apple spray that virtually no dog will find palatable. (If you use lemon juice or bitter apple, be very careful not to squirt it in or near your pup's eyes.)

The shake can is another dog-training tool that you can make at home: just take a clean soda can, drop five or six pennies in it, and tape the opening shut. It should make a noisy, ear-grating rattle when you shake it. You'll use this unpleasant little device to rattle some sense into your pup's brain when she gets mischievous.

But take note: Some people have a little too much fun with their bottles and cans, spraying and rattling with such abandon that their dogs soon either ignore the squirts and sounds entirely or grow frightened and nervous. So use them sparingly and judiciously, or don't use them at all. And don't get into the common habit of wielding them threateningly at your dog. In fact, it's best if she never even sees them; if you brandish them at her, they'll lose their element of surprise, and she'll soon figure out that she only needs to behave when you're armed.

Training treats. We're not above using a little bribery to get what we want. But we do mean *a little;* you don't want to turn your pup into a manipulative creature who utterly ignores you unless you wave a treat in front of her nose. (How many of your friends have dogs who will "do anything as long as we give her a treat"?) Anything your dog really enjoys will work as a training treat, as long as it's not too big and not too unhealthful. Broken-up biscuits, freeze-dried liver flakes, breakfast cereals or small chunks of apple are favorites of lots of dogs and their teachers; your dog will let you know whether she has a preference. (By the way, some dogs just aren't turned on by treats, and that's fine too.)

Your voice. This is the most important tool of all. If your dog learns to respect what you say and how you say it, then you've got a training tool that you'll never be without. Practice using different tones of voice to communicate exactly what you mean: a low, gruff tone to express displeasure (we like to use the ugly guttural sound *"Ah-ah!"* instead of "No," since "no" is such a mundane and ordinary-sounding word); a high, chirpy, happy tone to express delight when your pup does something wonderful; a calm, soothing tone to reassure your dog when she's unsure of herself. You should be able to get a physical reaction from your dog just by speaking to her in these different manners. For example, a good harsh "Ah-ah!" will make her look at you in startlement, while a few words of silly high-pitched praise should set her tail a-wagging. Don't yell at her; her ears are sensitive enough already. Don't shriek at her; high-pitched, frantic scolding will only convince her that you're not in control. Just be cool and collected, and she'll melt at the sound of your voice.

Your Dog's First Words

"Words, words, words," said Hamlet in disgust, and that's how your dog may start to think if you try to augment her vocabulary too rapidly in these first few days. We aren't going to introduce you to all the exercises she'll eventually need to learn, because that's best done in an obedience class; a book simply can't teach you to read and respond to your dog as well as a good instructor can. But we'll at least get you started with two important basic activities: *sit* and *let's go*. After all, we're going to give you tips on how to teach your dog *not* to do a handful of bothersome things, so we may as well teach her a couple of *yes's* to balance the *no's*. You don't want her to grow up thinking that education is just the process of learning all the things she's not allowed to do!

Sit

This is a great first exercise for you and your dog to learn: it's not too tough to master, so it's a good introduction to dog education for both of you, and it'll be wonderfully useful throughout your life together. Later in this chapter, we'll suggest that you use "sit" as a follow-up to many of the behavioral corrections you'll give your pup, since it will help her calm down and collect her thoughts, and it will give you a chance to praise her for doing the right thing. We like to use "sit" as a prerequisite to getting treats or supper, too, and it's a big help when you're going in or out of the house and don't want your dog to dash through the door.

Pick an appropriate time and place to begin teaching "sit." The best time to train your dog is when she's a little bit tired and a little bit hungry, and when *you're* nice and energetic and well-fed. Find a quiet room or a plot in the back yard, and a quiet five or ten minutes; kids running around, phones ringing, pots on the stove to tend to and other dogs eavesdropping will not make for an especially favorable learning environment. By the way, don't try to teach "sit" on a slippery floor, or your pooch's paws will keep oozing out from under her, and it will be a frustrating experience all around!

If your dog is an adult or an older puppy, she should be on her leash and training collar; if she's not yet used to this gear, keep her umbilical-corded for a few more days until she is. First, spend a moment stroking her, talking softly to her, and relaxing her. If she's hyper or nervous, or if she senses that *you're* hyper or nervous, you'll have a tough time maneuvering her into a sit. If your dog is a young pup or a submissive or shy dog, you'll probably be better off using her buckle collar.

Begin with your dog at your left side (you can stand or kneel depending on her size), with her leash gathered into your left hand and your right hand grasping the leash down by her collar, where the snap is. Now, three things have to happen at once. First, your left hand—still holding the leash, for security—has to scoop her rump into a sitting position. Second, your right hand has to pull up sharply on the leash. Third, you have to say—in your most authoritative tone of voice, even if you're feeling a little frazzled by all this activity—"Sit." And finally, when

The proper position for teaching the sit.

your dog is sitting (and that means *sitting*, not lying down or getting up again), you'll tell her what a wonderful girl she is and how proud you are of her.

Now we can back up and look at that whole process in a bit more detail. The job of your hands, obviously, is to get your dog to sit. The left one pulls straight up to pop the training collar, tightening it just for an instant, while the right one scoops the dog's rear underneath her. Don't push straight down on her hindquarters; not only can you damage a growing dog's joints that way, but you'll probably find that she'll lock her legs and refuse to sit. Slide your hand down and back from her rump and catch her behind the "knees," though, and she'll have no choice but to let her back legs fold under her. And don't be too dainty: make just one quick, firm, suave motion, and it'll be over before your dog even knows what happened. If you do a lot of tugging, tapping or poking, your dog will probably do more squirming and jumping than sitting, and she'll start to doubt your dog-training abilities. A good rule of thumb is this: When you're teaching the sit, don't put your hands on her until you're ready to make her sit, and don't take your hands off her until she's sitting. The whole thing shouldn't take more than a couple of seconds, unless your dog makes a really tricky move on you, which she probably will once in a while.

As for your "sit" command, give it in a deep, businesslike tone of voice just as your dog's rump is about to hit the ground, and—we'll say this more than once—*say* it only once! "Never repeat a command" is one of the cardinal rules of dog education, and new dog trainers are notorious for breaking it. When you say "Sit . . . sit . . . *sit* . . . PLEASE SIT" to your dog before actually getting her to sit, you're effectively teaching her that the first three commands didn't mean anything, and that she doesn't really need to take you seriously until you've repeated yourself several times and raised your voice. You want a dog who responds to your instructions the *first* time you deliver them, *every time.* (Think about it: If you have a teenager who knows that you'll tell him five times to clean his room before you take away his allowance, is he going to clean it the first time you ask or wait for the fifth?)

So you must resolve that throughout your dog's education, every command from you will result in a response from her. In the early stages of training, that means that you'll have to show her what you want when you say a word to her. Even after she begins to understand your commands, she may choose to ignore them on occasion, and instead of repeating yourself, you'll correct her immediately for her negligence.

Therefore, a corollary to the "Never repeat a command" rule is "Never give a command you can't enforce." (Memorize these little edicts now, and you'll be a standout in your obedience class.) Don't try to teach your dog "sit" when she's across the room from you or off her leash; be right on top of her, ready to help her do exactly what's expected of her, and she'll learn quickly.

When you praise her for a successful sit, don't get too excited, or she'll leap right up and forget that her sitting had anything to do with your newfound good mood. Stroke her head and back gently, and speak to her in your sweetest, calmest, happiest voice. Once in a while, you can even slip her a tiny, tiny treat for a particularly pretty sit—but don't overdo it.

Teaching "sit" to a small puppy is a slightly different monster. Puppies have shorter attention spans than older dogs, and they may take a bit longer to grasp things, but the commands they learn as youngsters will stay with them for a lifetime (provided you keep practicing!). Puppy bodies can be a little squirmy or squishy, which makes them hard to maneuver, but they're also small enough that they won't overpower you.

You can use a toned-down version of the just-described method on your puppy: Kneel on the floor beside her, and use your right hand to pull up gently on her leash and buckle collar while your right hand helps her rump down to the ground and you say "Sit." Then let her know how special and good she is.

Ten or twelve good sits are plenty for one training session during these early days. Too many repetitions will get boring; too few won't get your point across. Spend a good five minutes on "sit," then take a break and do three or four five-minute sessions throughout the day. If you're consistent with your training and genuine with your praise, your dog will probably have some understanding of the word within a few days. But don't hold her to that. Some dogs pick up the concept almost immediately; that's fantastic, but don't get overconfident—it will still take time for her to become really reliable. Other dogs seem to take forever to learn to sit on command, and that's okay too. Just keep up the repetitions and don't get impatient, and she'll catch on.

Ready for a new exercise? Here's one you'll both enjoy . . .

Let's go!

This is the phrase you'll use to go walking with your new dog. Notice that we aren't going to start out with "heel"; that's a more specific,

A brisk pace, a loose lead, and cheerful chatter are the keys to leash-walking. Jessica's smiling and Sebastian's wagging—just the way things ought to be.

demanding exercise that you'll learn when you go to school. "Let's go" is more informal. To your dog, it means that she must walk at your left side and in the direction you want to go, without pulling ahead or to the side, lagging behind or crowding you. To you, it means that you can take her for a walk without having to tug on her leash, trip over her or worry about what she's getting into with every step. You can use "let's go" any time you take your dog out on the town.

At some point in your dog-loving life, you've probably walked an untrained pooch—a rambunctious, sidewalk-hogging pup who pulled you in a thousand different directions and left you exhausted at the end of your excursion. Think back: Remember where her eyes were? Chances are, they were on everything except you. Likewise, her mind was on everything except you. If she'd been watching you, she really couldn't have gone very far astray, and that's where *your* dog is going to be different! Here's another rule to add to your list: There's no such thing as dog training without dog *attention.*

Your biggest, toughest job as you teach your pup to walk on a leash will be convincing her that you are more worthy of her attention than anything else going on around her. That includes other dogs and cats, mail carriers and fire hydrants, all of which are pretty interesting to a dog. In order to compete, you'll probably want to have a ball, a squeaky or jingly toy or a small stuffed animal to carry with you as you walk. Other than that, the only equipment you'll need is your ever-present leash and collar (chain for an adult dog, buckle for a puppy or a timid dog).

This doesn't mean, of course, that your dog can never again stop and sniff the flowers or visit a tree on your walks. It just means that you can use "let's go" to let her know when she needs to be at your side and paying attention.

Start your "let's go" training in a relatively distraction-free setting: your yard, maybe, or a dull stretch of sidewalk. Have your dog on her collar and leash. Before you go anywhere, get her interested in the toy you've brought with you. Show it to her and let her know how delightful it is: "What's this?" you can ask her. "Don't you want to get this wonderful toy?" If she's not really turned on, go find something else that's more enticing to her (and be creative; one of our dogs, for example, is mistrustful of squeakies and unexcited by rubber balls but will do anything for a dried leaf). Don't start walking until her attention is riveted on whatever you've got in your hand.

When she's hooked, stand with her at your left side; gather most of her leash in your right hand (fold it up accordion-style), and keep your left hand on the leash close to her collar. Your left hand also has the duty of holding the toy, and squeaking or jingling it if necessary. Your hands should stay down near your waist and close to your body as you walk; flailing arms leave you unbalanced and unable to direct your dog's movements. And your body should remain upright; don't bend over when you give leash corrections or squeak your toy, or you'll end up with a bad back and a bewildered dog.

When you're ready to step off, give a loud, cheerful "Let's go!" command and start walking. Use your voice (keep it high-pitched, happy and chatty) and your toy to keep your pup's eyes on you and her tail wagging. Keep the leash *loose* between you; your pup should never feel her collar tighten unless she's getting a correction.

Start with just a few steps. If you turn your very first "let's go" session into a cross-country jaunt, your dog will get bored and stop watching you. Keep talking to her and flashing her toy every few seconds, but make sure your chatter and your squeaking or jingling don't get monotonous, or they'll lose their effect.

And move *briskly!* Don't let your dog slow you down, and don't hang around waiting for her if she's dragging her feet. You should keep moving at a fast walk—the way you'd walk if it were raining and cold and you didn't have your umbrella. Let your dog know that you find leash-walking to be the most thrilling, exhilarating activity in the world, and you're certain she'll share your opinion.

But guess what? She probably *won't* share your opinion just yet, not all of the time. She may want to head off in another direction, or she may try to wind her leash around you, or she may stop cold and refuse to go any farther. Don't be impatient. Remember, she may never have been walked by anyone before, and the whole thing is pretty confusing to her right now. If she pulls away from you, give her a little pop on the leash—not a head-ripping haul or a dull tug, but a clean, quick jerk—in the direction she ought to be moving. (Don't make the common mistake of jerking *up* on her leash—you aren't trying to teach her to fly, after all!) Follow your leash pop with a sweet "Oh, weren't you watching?" or "What happened?" Slowly she'll begin to learn that it's to her advantage to watch where you're going.

If she darts away from you or tries to walk on your right side or in front or back of you, there's probably too much leash between you. Move your left hand closer to her collar and try again.

If she curls up on the ground and acts as though you're torturing her—and shelter dogs sometimes do—you'll have to do some sweet-talking. *Don't* coddle her or pet her when she's cowering (you don't want to reward her and make this a habit), but don't be too hard on her, either, and for Pete's sake don't try to yank her off the ground. Try to "jolly her up" with your voice and your body language; tell her she's a big, brave girl, and project an air of cheer and confidence to her. Use her toy—or even a treat if necessary—to coax her to her feet. It may take a while, but if you're patient and good-natured, you'll be able to change her attitude.

After eight or ten good, quick steps—that means that your dog stayed at your left side, watched you and didn't pull on her leash more than once or twice—stop and celebrate. Now, unlike during your "sit" practice, you can go a little crazy. Then ride the excitement of the moment: Give another "Let's go!" and take a few more steps!

Keep praising your dog for her attention and enthusiasm and correcting her for her lapses. Gradually increase the distance you walk, and start making turns and circles to add some variety and challenge. Take her to different places with more distractions; use your "let's

Don't forget to end every training session with a hug!

go" command when you're walking in the park or through town. And when you sign up your dog and yourself for obedience school, you'll have a terrific head start on heeling (and you'll also be able to stroll smartly into class on the first night without your dog dragging you through the door!).

Mischief-Making and How to Manage It

Most shelter dogs come with some ready-made behavior problems, and those that don't will usually develop a few out of sheer ingenuity. And the stress of adapting to a new living situation and a new family is especially likely to bring out new bad habits or exacerbate old ones. Don't panic, and don't take it personally; your dog isn't doing anything unusual, incurable, or ungrateful. She's not being "bad" out of spite, so don't correct her in spite; your goal is to stop her improper behavior calmly and authoritatively, not to get revenge. Remember, she may never have had to abide by anyone's rules before, but that doesn't mean she can't learn yours.

We've listed a few of the more common doggie problems here, but a few overriding principles apply to all of them:

- *Don't ask for trouble.* If you know your dog likes to chew your socks or dig in your plants, don't leave your socks and plants where she can reach them just yet. If she only causes trouble when she's left unsupervised, don't leave her unsupervised until she's trustworthy. In other words, give her as few chances as possible to be bad during these early weeks. But don't go overboard and lock her in her crate all day, either; that's not fair to her, and besides, she'll never learn if she's never allowed to make mistakes.

- *Be consistent at all costs.* We've said it before, but it bears repeating: Set rules, and stick to them. Correct your dog every time she errs, not just when it's convenient (and not just when you happen to catch her—which means you need to oversee her activities constantly at the beginning). And hold a family meeting to make sure that everyone in the household is correcting the same problems in the same way; don't let anybody try to play the "good cop" by being soft on your pup's uncouth behaviors. That won't earn anybody points; it will just result in a very confused and unmannered dog.

- *Catch her in the act, or don't catch her at all.* Just as in house-breaking, you have to correct a mistake *as* it's happening, not a minute or an hour later. You can scold your dog if you find her chewing up your favorite book, but not if you find your favorite book chewed up on the floor and no dog in sight. If you wait too long to make the correction, she'll have many happy memories of eating your book and no idea that your anger is in any way related to it. Guess what that means? Yep. Supervision.

- *Entrapment isn't illegal in dog training.* Suppose you're having trouble catching your dog in the act of stealing food from your countertops. Why not set her up? Leave some irresistible tidbit where she can see it, and be ready to correct her with your shake can or spray bottle and your sharp voice when she goes for the goods. Cheating? Maybe—but it works. Don't forget to tell her when she's good. You don't want to be a nay-sayer all the time; if you've told her she's naughty for pouncing on your petunias, then tell her she's terrific when you see her resisting the urge to do so. If you don't temper your corrections with praise, she's going to start feeling frustrated and downtrodden rather than secure and happy in the knowledge that she's a responsible, trusted family member.

- *Exercise and educate.* It may seem as though your dog has a million different troublesome behaviors, each more puzzling or frustrating than the last. Maybe it will make you feel better to know that practically all her misdemeanors can be attributed to two simple problems: boredom and lack of respect for you. The cure for boredom is regular exercise; the cure for lack of respect is ongoing education. It's as easy as that.

Here's an alphabetical list of a few of the behavior problems shelter dogs most frequently bring home with them; if your dog comes up with some ingenious problems of her own, you can probably come up with some ingenious solutions to them by using your arsenal of information and training tools, and by exercising and educating your dog now and throughout her life.

Barking. We'll start right in with a tough one. Actually, it's easy enough to stop your dog from barking when you're right next to her: just clamp your hand around her snout, hooking your finger into the little soft spot under her chin—this is called a *muzzle squeeze,* by the way,

Learn to give a firm muzzle squeeze; it will come in handy.

and it's useful in lots of situations—and say "Quiet!" sharply. When she stops barking, stroke her and tell how good she is to hold her tongue. If you consistently pair the muzzle squeeze with the command, she'll eventually learn to pipe down upon hearing the word "quiet" by itself.

You can use your spray bottle to curb barking, too: when your pup gets talkative, aim a stream of water or lemon juice at her mouth and say "Quiet!" She'll learn that when she hears that word, she'd best keep her mouth shut.

Unfortunately, most problem barking happens when you're not around and your dog is bored and lonesome. Crating her while you're away should help in the beginning (but not for too long at a stretch), and keeping your goodbyes calm and unemotional will also make her less apt to fret when she sees you heading out. And you may be able to keep her content in your absence by leaving her a special toy or chew, or a radio playing. If possible, give her some exercise before you leave the house so that she'll be more likely to fall asleep than to bark nervously when you go.

If you know that she's likely to start creating a ruckus a few minutes after your departure, then set her up: put on your coat, pick up your briefcase or backpack, and pretend to leave, but wait quietly outside the door instead, not close enough that she can hear or smell you, but close enough that you'll hear her if she makes a fuss. If she barks, rush headlong back into the house or apartment and surprise her with a muzzle squeeze, a loud "Quiet!" command and your best air of disgust and displeasure. (She was barking to get you to come back to her, but this isn't the reception she'd hoped for.) Then leave again, and keep ambushing her as long as she keeps barking. When she's finally quiet, go back inside and praise her sweetly; she'll figure out that you like to come home to a quiet dog.

By the way, don't worry that you may be teaching your dog never to bark at all. She'll still let you know when a burglar or a pizza-delivery person comes to the door, but you'll be able to use your "quiet" command to let *her* know when enough is enough.

Begging. It's difficult to cure begging but much less so to prevent it: If you never, ever feed your dog from the table, she'll learn never to expect anything, but if you slip her treats on the sly every once in a while, then she'll always hold out hope. So tell your family not to treat your dog from the table, and don't give her tidbits when you're snacking or preparing food, either. When you do give her dog treats, require her to sit first, and don't feed her on demand. In other words, make sure *you're* in control of when, where, and how much you feed her. When you take her to obedience school, she'll learn how to do a down-stay, and you can have her do this during dinnertime every evening.

Chewing. Chewing is probably neck-and-neck with barking as the number-one mischievous thing dogs do when their people are away. Puppies chew when they're cutting teeth; adolescents chew when they get their grown-up teeth; practically all dogs chew when they're bored or nervous. The first thing to do, as we've already noted, is to get any prized chewable possessions out of your dog's reach just so you won't spend your whole workday worrying that she's gnawing on your new tennis racket or your collected works of Shakespeare. The second thing to do is to make sure she has a selection of her *own* toys to munch on. But beware: if you leave *too* many doggie playthings lying around, she may start to think that every mouth-sized object she finds around the house is a toy for her. It's better for her to have several special items that she'll recognize as her own. (If she has a whole slew of toys, you can rotate them and leave two or three available at a time; that will also help prevent her from getting bored with her playthings.)

If you catch your dog chewing on something that isn't hers, get the object out of her mouth by squeezing the sides of her muzzle until she releases it. If she's got her teeth really tightly clamped around it and refuses to let go, try blowing very quickly and sharply into her ear or aiming a squirt of lemon juice or bitter apple at her mouth; she'll probably release her grip long enough for you to grab her goodie. (This is all a whole lot easier to do if she's umbilical-corded to you, by the way, since her first reaction may be to engage you in a game of keep-away). Give her a muzzle squeeze and a good harsh "Ah-ah!" After she's duly chastened, find her an acceptable toy, and praise her lavishly for chewing it.

Can you find the naughty dog in this picture? She's under the dresser, wishing she hadn't chewed up that roll of toilet paper.

Suppose she does most of her chewing when you're gone. Again, the best solution may be to crate her or keep her in a dog-proofed room until she's kicked her chewing habit. Or, if you know that she has certain favorite items to destroy, spritz them with bitter apple, which is safe to spritz on most surfaces (there's even a special formula for plants). If your dog happens to put her mouth on a chair leg or a begonia that's been bitter-appled, she'll probably make a terrible face and a mental note not to return. (It may take a few tries, though, so don't give up.)

Digging. Tilling the soil is a natural doggie habit, but it's one you may not appreciate if it takes place in your vegetable garden or your houseplants. If possible, fence off forbidden areas in your yard, and elevate, cover or lace with bitter apple or cayenne pepper your indoor plants.

You might consider giving your dog a special digging place of her own—a little plot of ground or a wooden tub of dirt where she *is* allowed to scrabble around—so that she won't be so tempted to do so in your flowers.

If you haven't already asked your vet to show you how to cut your dog's toenails, now is the time to do so. Digging with trimmed nails doesn't feel nearly as nice as digging with long, unclipped claws.

Bean and Tripod know how to play together nicely, but if your two dogs get too rough, you'll have to step in.

You can use your shake can or spray bottle if you catch your dog in the act of digging; try not to let her see what you're up to, then surprise her with a metallic rattle or a blast of water. But for a dog who digs when she's left alone in the yard, supervision and setups are in order. Put her on a leash and turn her loose in the yard as usual, but watch her from a window, and race out the door to yank her away and give her a loud "Ah-ah!" if you catch her working the earth.

There's one more highly effective way to discourage digging; you'll need your pooper scooper for this one. Find a spot in the yard where your dog likes to dig, and fill it with a shallow layer of her own stools (collect them from the yard; it's okay if they're a few days old). Cover them up with dirt, and wait until your dog digs there again; chances are, she'll be unpleasantly surprised to discover the treasure you've left her, and she'll think twice about digging there again. You can use this strategy in all her favorite spots, and before long she'll decide that digging really isn't worth the trouble.

Fighting with other dogs. Adopted dogs may not be accustomed to having canine roommates, and it's not unusual to have a few spats when you first introduce your dog to her new doggie step-siblings. Sometimes it takes only a couple of scuffles for them to determine who's the top dog, but sometimes the fighting continues, and that's when you need to step in. Normal canine play usually includes some wrestling and scuffling, which is nothing to worry about, but when friendly grumbles give way to curled-lip snarls and biting, things have gone too far.

Rule number one: *Don't* get between two fighting dogs! There's a good chance that you'll get bitten and they'll go right on battling. If they're wearing their leashes, you may be able to pull them apart with someone else's help. If you have a garden hose or a faucet spray nozzle handy, you may be able to soak them into a détente. Otherwise, your best bet is to aim your spray bottle of lemon juice at their mouths and distract them with its sharp taste. Once they're separated, read them both the riot act (unless one was clearly the aggressor and the other was a passive victim—but it usually takes two to tangle). Grab them by the scruffs of their necks, hold their muzzles shut, and tell them in a deep, stern voice that you'll have no fighting in your home. When they've calmed down a bit, leash them and give them a chance to approach each other slowly and calmly, and praise them for their civility.

Don't inadvertently encourage competition between your dogs. Give them their own toys, crates and bowls; feed them separately; and don't "play favorites" since dogs notice that sort of thing. Discourage tug-of-war or other combative games between them. If the problem continues, you will have to consult a professional obedience trainer who can see the situation firsthand and offer you some solutions. With dogs as with kids, sibling rivalry is to be expected, but you mustn't let the jealousy and competitiveness reach disruptive or dangerous levels.

Getting on furniture. Before your dog ever enters your home, decide what pieces of furniture, if any, she'll be allowed to sit on. She can learn that the sofa is off-limits while the easy chair is okay, but she *can't* learn that the sofa is okay as long as you don't have company over, or that the easy chair is off-limits unless it gets cold and you want her warm body next to you. Make a decision and stand by it, and make sure that she has her own cozy bed—whether it's a monogrammed cedar-filled cushion by the fireplace or an old folded-up blanket in her crate—so that she won't be quite so tempted to invade *your* space.

When your dog is umbilical-corded, it's easy to correct her for getting on forbidden furniture: when she starts to hop up on your lounge chair or loveseat, give her a leash-jerk back down to earth, and say "Off!" ("Off"—not "down," since that will mean "lie down" later in your training—is the magic word to use whenever your pup's paws are where you don't want them to be.) Then show her her own bed or her crate, and praise her if she chooses to lie on it, or have her sit and praise her for complying.

Your shake can will be handy as well, if you can sneak up behind your pup as she attempts to get comfy on an off-limits piece of furniture. The key is to catch her in the act of climbing on the furniture, not after she's been snoozing happily on the couch for twenty minutes, or else she may decide that the nice nap is worth the eventual correction.

Some dogs get on the furniture only when their people aren't around. (We know a couple whose Weimaraner wasn't allowed in the living room chair; they never, ever caught him lounging in the chair, but its seat cushion was usually warm when they got home.) You can probably outsmart such behavior by booby-trapping your furniture: Leave some inflated balloons on the couch, or a couple of noisy pots or pans on the easy chair. Your dog will soon realize that her crate or doggie bed is by far the best seat in the house.

Guarding food or objects. Remember, your dog's ancestors were pack animals who had to protect their possessions from the other canines if they wanted to survive. Your sweet pup doesn't need to get proprietary with you, but that urge may still run deep in her, and you'll have to convince her that it's neither necessary nor acceptable. But there are two sides to this deal: since you expect her not to defend her toys and food from you, you also need to let her know that you're not going to taunt her by taking away her things unfairly or disturbing her unnecessarily during dinnertime (after all, you don't want her begging while *you're* eating!). So teach your family—especially little children—that they're not allowed to tease your dog when she's busy with a toy or a meal, and teach *her* that she's not allowed to growl or snarl at you if you ever really do need to take something (like a toy or tidbit that isn't hers or could be dangerous) away from her.

If your dog has some prized possession in her mouth and growls at you when you approach, get tough, or this could be the start of some very bad habits. Don't try to grab the object from her, since she'll probably take off or snap at you; instead, give her a nasty "Ah-ah," and get your spray bottle of lemon juice or bitter apple, and aim a stream of it at her mouth. She'll either drop the object or be distracted enough that you can take it from her, scolding her in your deep, serious, I'm-disappointed-in-you voice as you do so. Keep the toy for a few minutes, and require her to sit for you before you give it back.

Mealtime can present problems, too, but you can help prevent them by giving your dog a quiet place and time to eat. If she growls when someone comes near her food bowl, you need to teach her that since *you* are the one dishing out the grub, you're also the one who has the right to take it away if necessary. Instead of putting a full food bowl in front of her, start feeding her a little at a time; let her eat one handful of food, and wait a few seconds before giving her the next one.

Some dogs get territorial about furniture, and that's another habit that *must* be halted, even though people sometimes find it cute at first. Even if it initally seems charming that your pup loves your sofa enough to growl about it, it'll be scary later on if she becomes aggressive when someone wants to take a seat next to her. Even if your dog is allowed on the furniture, teach her the command "off" (described in the section on getting on furniture), and use it to be certain that she'll vacate your chair or couch on request. If at *any* time she growls at you when you ask her to move or when you try to join her, she loses her furniture privileges. Period. She can earn them back in the future, after she's been to obedience school and proven that she knows she's not the boss, but for now she can stick to her own bed and the floor. It may sound harsh, but remember the Lhasa Apso who terrorized her whole family one morning by not letting anybody get on or off the bed? Well, he started small!

Above all, get your dog and yourself to obedience class. Possessiveness is a clear indication that your dog isn't yet convinced that she owes you her respect. That has to change, and it can!

Jumping on people. Dogs who leap on people are annoying, but people who let them get away with it are even more so! Even if *you* don't mind having dog paws on you, you can't be sure that all your guests will feel the same way, or that you won't change your mind when you've got your best suit or stockings on. Conversely, if you're

A no-jumping correction: Sam didn't intend for her paws to get stuck in the air when she jumped on Jessica!

trying to teach your dog not to jump, you need to make sure your visitors don't allow—or, worse, *encourage*—jumping. Consistency is a must. Perhaps you've heard us say that before.

The three worst things you can do to a dog who jumps on you are (1) slam her in the chest with your knee; (2) step on her toes; or (3) pet her. The first two methods (which you may have heard recommended as cures for jumping) could hurt her, and they'll certainly make her afraid of you. And the third crime—the one we're most likely to commit—will just teach her to keep on leaping.

There are two ways to correct a jumping dog: one that involves a leash and one that doesn't. If your dog is on her leash and takes a leap at you, quickly grasp the leash close to her collar, give her a sharp snap *downwards,* and say "Off!" in a tone of voice that means business. (Again, don't use the word "down," since that's going to have its own meaning when you go to obedience class.) Then—and this is crucial!—give her a "Sit" command and make sure she does it. Once she's sitting, *then* you may pet her. Her objective in jumping, after all, was to get your attention and affection; she needs to learn that she won't get it when she's in the air but she *will* get it when she sits nicely in front of you, even if that arrangement seems contrary to her canine logic.

If your dog's on-leash and she jumps on somebody else, it's your job to give her a sharp jerk backwards and downwards and an "Off!" command. And ask your friends and family to cooperate with you by never rewarding your dog for jumping. This is an ideal situation for a setup: have a friend tempt your pup to jump on him or her, and you be ready to give a correction with your leash and your voice. As always, follow up with a "Sit" and a hearty dose of praise; and when she begins to resist the temptation to jump (or, even better, starts to sit automatically for praise), reward her self-restraint will lots of petting and gushing. Since most jumping problems are at their worst when people come to the door, keep a leash by your door and snap it onto your pup's collar when visitors arrive so that you'll be ready to correct her.

But what if your dog isn't on her leash when she decides to jump on you? You can still give her a correction, but you have to be swift: while she's on her hind legs, grab her front paws and hold them up in the air, as in the photo. Don't squeeze them hard; just hold them as if you were about to start waltzing. Sooner or later, she'll start to worry that she may never get down again, and she'll probably start pulling away from you or whining. This, after all, was hardly what she'd planned; she was looking for a pat on the head, and instead her paws have gotten mysteriously stuck in the air. At this point, wait a few more seconds, and then let her go and end with the obligatory "sit." This is an easy and remarkably effective method of curbing jumping; you'll see that after two or three paw-holds in a row, she'll probably decide to keep four feet on the floor (for which you will, of course, praise her liberally), and after a few days, if you and your family are consistent, she'll start to have second thoughts about jumping in general. (One of us was once told by a friend, "I think the best thing I've ever gotten out of our friendship was that paws-in-the-air method of teaching my dog not to jump; it really works!")

Nipping and snapping. Hear this: *At no time* is it okay for your dog to put her teeth on any part of a human body. Nipping and mouthing are not acceptable, not even from little puppies. Remember that puppy teeth may not hurt very much, but they'll soon fall out and be replaced with adult ones that will. So don't *ever* encourage your dog to nibble or teethe on you, and don't play games (like "jump up to grab the toy/treat in my hand") that encourage her to nip at you. Teach your small children to keep their hands away from her mouth.

When you do feel doggie teeth on you, don't take it lightly; let your pup know that even if she meant no harm, this is a behavior you won't tolerate. Give her a muzzle squeeze and a harsh "Ah-ah!" For extra effect, you can grasp the fold of skin behind her neck and give her a little shake. Be sure to clasp her snout tightly, hooking your finger below her chin so that she can't pull away. When you feel her relaxing, release her slowly, and be ready to do it again if she nips again. Once her urge to nip or snap has passed, praise her for being such a sweet girl.

We're not going to say too much about more serious aggression because that's a problem that needs to be addressed one-on-one with an in-home professional trainer. An aggression problem doesn't mean that your dog is evil or that you chose her unwisely; it just means she has to understand that she's not the top dog in your home, and that she's not allowed to use her teeth to express her opinions about whom she likes and whom she doesn't. If your dog bites, you *must* consult your obedience instructor or another trainer who can work with you privately, or the situation will only get worse. If you haven't had your aggressive dog spayed or neutered yet, do so immediately. In the meantime, you've got to get tough with her and let her know in no uncertain terms that you're the boss, and you will not put up with biting or any other form of disrespect. Supervise her constantly, require her to sit for you before she gets any treats or toys, feed her a handful at a time, and—in short—don't let her call any of the shots. Aggression isn't uncommon, and it *is* treatable, but it will demand that you and your family turn your home into something of a military school for your pup while you're getting help from a pro.

   Stealing food and objects. We know a goofy Lab who used to drive his family crazy by picking up a knick-knack and running pell-mell around the house with it, encouraging everyone to join him in a wild and crazy game of chase. The solution was simple: they let him wear his leash around the house, and when he stole something, it was easy to catch him and take it away. No game, no fun, no more stealing. Try this on your pup if she's become a thief; just be sure you're watching her so that her leash doesn't get caught on anything.

   To remove an object or a piece of food from your dog's mouth, act fast, before she's had a chance to enjoy it: grab her snout from the top with one hand and squeeze inward on the sides (pressing on her upper gums and teeth), and with the other hand reach in and extract the goods. Use the word "Out" or "Give," then praise her when she releases her grip. If she's really tenacious, hold her head still and blow very quickly and sharply in her ear; she'll unclench her jaws for a moment, and you can snatch away her prize.

   You can use your bitter apple to prevent stealing, too. Set up your dog by leaving a piece of her favorite pilferable food in her favorite pilfering place, but lace it with a spray of bitter apple or a dash of cayenne pepper (not too much, please!), and then stand back and watch your dog learn that crime doesn't pay.

Formal Education

Education begins at home, but it doesn't end there. It's important that you supplement your dog's home schooling with a good obedience class—or several! Why is obedience school so necessary? Well, here's a starter list:

- ***You and your dog will learn more advanced commands.*** You've got a good start with "sit" and "let's go," but in class you'll master exercises like "down," "stay," "heel," "stand" and "come" as well—the vocabulary she'll need to become a really responsive and trustworthy friend and partner.

- *Your instructor can address your specific needs.* Books and videotapes are great, but they can't stay after class to discuss your dog's individual problems or strong points, they can't demonstrate new moves to you, and they can't tell you whether you're holding your leash funny or giving your dog a confusing command. There's really no substitute for the one-on-one attention and suggestions of a good instructor.

- *You'll learn from the other people and dogs in the class.* Your classmates may have new ideas for you, or you may pick up tips just from watching them. And you'll find that they're sympathetic to your problems and proud of your successes in ways that your non-dog-loving friends may not be. (That's why we nickname our obedience classes "doggie support groups!")

- *Your dog will get used to other people and dogs.* This is a biggie. No amount of backyard practice can teach your dog to behave in the presence of other exciting people or pups. And if your adopted dog is still a little worried about the world at large—and many of them are—obedience class will give her a chance to make friends and gain confidence. So even if you've already been through obedience class with another dog and know the ropes, it's a good idea to take your new dog to a class of her own.

- *It'll give you an incentive to train your dog.* Let's face it: sometimes it's tough to get motivated for your daily training sessions when you know only a couple of exercises and you don't have an instructor and classmates to keep you from getting lazy!

- *You'll have a terrific time.* Obedience class is fun! You'll make new friends (we know several married couples who met in obedience class!) and get lots of exercise, and your relationship with your new dog will soar to new levels. And who knows? You might just get hooked on dog training and find yourself with a new hobby. It happens, trust us. . . .

It's not hard to find an obedience class to attend—they're available all over the country, all year round—but these days, training classes and training methods come in so many varieties that it's important to know what you're getting into before you fork over your tuition. Here are a few of the most common kinds of training classes you're likely to find in your area:

"Hello, do you offer puppy classes?"

Puppy classes. Sometimes called "puppy kindergarten," puppy classes are designed for dogs under four or five months old, and they're the newest addition to the obedience-class family. A few decades ago, it was believed that dogs couldn't do any useful learning until they were at least six months old, but we know now that that's bunk, and that young puppies make great students and retain what they learn extremely well. If you've adopted a small pup, we wholeheartedly, enthusiastically recommend that you take her to a puppy class, where the two of you will probably learn basic commands like "sit," "down," "stay," "come" and some variation on "let's go." You may also learn some simple games ("fetch," maybe) and household exercises (like "go to your bed" or "wait at the door"), and you should receive useful information about your pup's health, grooming and housebreaking. And puppy class will help build your pup's confidence and broaden her horizons during the first and most formative weeks of her life.

Basic obedience classes. Most training classes are of this sort—they're aimed at dogs of at least five or six months of age who lack basic manners. You don't need to have had any previous training to take a class like this, though you'll find it goes more smoothly if you've had the opportunity to attend a puppy class. You'll learn exercises like "sit," "down," "stay," "heel," "stand" and "come," and you'll address common canine problems like jumping or nipping. A basic training class is a must for every dog. Your pup will learn some useful etiquette, and you'll earn her respect and establish yourself as her leader. Most beginning classes stick to on-leash training, though many do introduce limited off-leash work toward the end of the course.

"Advanced basic" classes. Some training schools and clubs offer a separate class to teach you and your dog to work together off-leash; check with the instructors you call to find out exactly what each level of obedience class covers.

Competition classes. You may see advertisements for "Novice," "Open" and "Utility" classes; these are for dogs and people who have completed basic training and want to go on to do more advanced obedience work, usually with the goal of competing in Obedience Trials for titles or prizes. (Take note, though: sometimes "Novice" refers to a beginning obedience class, not to a competition class; make sure you know what you're getting if you sign up for a class by that name.) We'll talk more about advanced obedience training and Obedience Trials in Chapter 7.

Boarding school. Some training schools offer one- to six-week "residential" programs for dogs: you drop your dog off, and when you pick her up a few weeks later, she's trained. Sound like a neat deal? Well, it can be, but it has major drawbacks. For one thing, it's very expensive, since you're paying for one-on-one professional training as well as boarding costs. Boarding means not home, in cage, not good . . . . More importantly, it doesn't let you and your dog enjoy your education together; you won't learn how to teach and communicate with your dog if you let someone else do it for you. In cases of very serious behavior problems, boarding school may be a necessary option, but otherwise, we think you'll find that a training class is more educational, enjoyable and economical.

Canine Good Citizen classes and Agility classes. We'll talk about these in detail in the next chapter.

When you're ready to sign up your new buddy and yourself for an obedience class, scout around for trainers or training clubs in your area. Some training schools are independently owned businesses; some professional trainers offer classes privately; local kennel clubs or obedience training clubs usually hold classes with their members as instructors; and many YMCAs and large animal shelters offer obedience classes. Check your Yellow Pages under "Dog Training," look in the newspaper for advertisements of upcoming classes, ask your vet or the staff at the animal shelter to recommend local obedience trainers, and make a few phone calls.

We've talked in earlier chapters about large pet-supply places; many of them are also in the obedience-training business, often offering classes right in the aisles of the stores. As much as we like the stores, we don't necessarily recommend the classes, since the training space is often limited, slippery and filled with other canine customers and their noise and germs.

It shouldn't be too tough to find a class that will fit into your schedule; most are offered on weeknights, but daytime and Saturday classes are also available in most areas. Don't plan to start an obedience class if you know that your dog is due to be spayed or neutered while school's in session, since those operations require a few days to a week of rest. And be sure that *your* life isn't so hectic that you might have to miss classes or neglect your daily training sessions. Remember, you'll need to put in twenty or thirty minutes of homework every day if you really want to benefit from your obedience class. (Also, if you'll be doing most of your home practice outdoors, choose a time when the weather will be cooperative—not the dead of winter or the hottest days of summer.)

Cost is an issue too, of course. Most basic training classes cost between $30 and $125 for eight to ten weeks of instruction; puppy classes may run for fewer weeks and cost somewhat less. Tuition prices aren't always directly proportional to quality; they often reflect rent and overhead costs more than expertise. So don't immediately sign up for the cheapest class you find, but don't assume that the priciest is going to be the best, either.

Choosing an obedience class is a little like choosing a shelter, and it shouldn't be done in haste—not even if your dog is driving you crazy and you think you can't wait another minute to haul her off to school! Too many people sign up for the first class they find, not realizing that there's more than one way to train a dog, and that not every instructor or method is appropriate for every dog or dog-lover. And it's important to find an instructor who will understand the special needs of your adopted dog.

Don't enroll in an obedience class without first speaking to the instructor on the phone or—preferably—visiting a class. You want to find an instructor who makes you feel comfortable, someone friendly, knowledgeable, and genuinely interested in you and your dog, who has had experience working with all different kinds of people and dogs, including adopted dogs, and who will be willing and able to answer your questions both now and later. And you want a training method based on motivation, positive reinforcement and firm, fair corrections—not on force, fear, or bribery. Don't take your pup to an instructor who uses electric training collars or encourages excessively harsh and frequent physical corrections; there are much better ways to win your dog's respect and obedience.

When you visit a training class don't take your dog with you unless you've gotten the instructor's permission to do so. But do take your powers of observation and perhaps your ever-present notepad and pencil. There shouldn't be more than a dozen students in a single class, unless there's more than one instructor. And the training area should be large enough to accommodate everybody; it's very hard to train a dog in a cramped space with lots of other dogs around.

Watch how the instructor, the students and the dogs interact. Does everybody seem happy to be there? If a student is having problems with a particular exercise, does the instructor try to find out what's wrong and fix it? Above all, do you feel that you'd be comfortable learning from this instructor and using these training methods on your dog?

A good instructor and a good class, of course, is only half the bargain. Resolve that you're going to make the most of obedience school by going to every class, practicing at home every day, setting realistic goals and keeping your sense of humor. Promise yourself and your dog that you'll try not to get impatient or frustrated (even though you'll be tempted at times), and that you won't unfairly compare her to the other dogs in your class. There will be times when you'll think your dog is *never* going to catch on, days when you'd much rather watch tele-vision than practice your obedience exercises and embarrassing moments when your mischievous pup will make you feel silly in front of your classmates. But there will also be breakthroughs, sympathetic classmates to congratulate your successes and keep your setbacks in perspective, and lots of good times for you and your dog. Work hard and have fun.

Sandra Brown and Poppy
Santa Rosa, California

Photograph by Sharon Taussig

It was a dark and stormy night . . . oops, wrong story. Actually it was on a beautiful morning in June that I traveled to the local animal shelter to look for a companion for my Golden Retriever Mandy; I worked long shifts, and she was alone a lot. I almost didn't go that morning because of memories of earlier visits: the sad faces, the frantic "take me home" barking, the knowledge that I could take only one. But which one?

I'd almost finished looking when I noticed two Golden Retrievers in a kennel together. I knelt down and knew instantly that I had found my dog. One of the Goldens, a male, was the more demonstrative, licking my hand, wiggling, so happy to be touched. But it was the other one who caught my eye and my heart. She leaned against the enclosure, head bowed, quiet brown eyes fixed on me. I reached into the cage, and she placed a big soft paw in my hand and squeezed softly, then licked me. That was the start of a long and happy relationship.

I couldn't take her home for a few days, since there was a waiting period. The day I picked her up, my best friend, Debbie Stoner, met me at the shelter for moral support. (Why did I need moral support, for goodness sakes? I wasn't adopting a child—or was I?)

They brought Poppy to us in an enclosure so that she could meet Mandy. The two of them hit it off right away. Then the most wonderful thing happened: Poppy went over to Debbie, gently took her purse from her and returned to me. She slowly rose up on her hind legs, grasped my waist with her front legs and handed the purse to me. She wanted to give me a gift! Either that, or she was a purse snatcher in a previous life. If I'd had any doubts, they faded away in a heartbeat. She was mine!

When we got home that morning, she walked into the living room, started picking up Mandy's toys, then proceeded to hop on the sofa and sit regally, face full of stuffed, torn toys. I swear I heard her say "Okay— these are mine, the house is mine, the nice lady is mine. Mandy, go get your own!"

My affiliation with the Sonoma County Humane Society grew out of my adoption of Poppy. I wanted to repay them for my great companion, so we joined the Pet Therapy Program, in which volunteers and their pets visit elderly people in convalescent homes. Debbie and I later became coordinators of the program. Poppy has developed a reputation on her visits: She walks in, eyes an unsuspecting chair next to a senior citizen, gently climbs into it, and leans against the surprised patient and offers her paw. If she doesn't get stroked, she leans a bit more and looks at the patient as if to say "Hi—I'm here. Everything's fine. *Pet* me."

She had one special friend at a convalescent hospital; it was a short relationship, as Frank was dying of cancer. They met during a regular visit, when Frank was dozing upright on a couch. Next thing he knew, he had a seventy-pound dog draped across his lap. I remember his smile, and I can still hear him saying "Can she please stay with me? It's lonely here. She can sleep on my bed. She'd be no trouble at all." We saw Frank only one more time. We left a photo I had taken of him and Poppy on his pillow as we said goodbye.

Poppy and I also run Humane Society booths at fairs, march in parades and do P.R. and fundraising for the shelter. She's even allowed at the yearly banquet! She and I have received several awards: Volunteer of the Quarter, Volunteer of the Year and a citation for five years of outstanding service. She has a Versatile Canine Companion title and a Canine Good Citizen title. And she's brightened the lives of many people and encouraged them to adopt their pets from animal shelters. After all, I got a great pal that way, and others can, too!

These last six years would not have had the same meaning to me if Poppy hadn't come into my life. I've had the best friend a person could hope for, made many new friends, and had an effect on others' lives as a result of her gentle nature and beautiful soul.

The most difficult time we've gone through was the loss of my beloved Mandy to leukemia in August of 1994. Poppy was inconsolable, but she'd always been there for me, so now it was my turn to repay her. She still misses her friend, as do I, but maybe she and I will go back to that same shelter someday and give another dog like Poppy the chance to shine in the world.

CHAPTER 7

Life on the Outside

Dogs crave companionship, entertainment, guidance and exercise. Chances are your adopted pup didn't get as much of those as she deserved during her shelter days and before. Even the very best shelters, after all, have lots of dogs to tend to and seldom enough hours or employees to go around. And while your dog enjoyed the company of the shelter staff, she probably didn't have one special person to be her buddy and show her the ropes and tell her she was the best pup in the world.

But now she has you! Now the two of you can make up for lost time by going new places and trying new things together. You can introduce her to your friends and show her your world: take her for a jump in the leaves, a romp through the snow, a walk through town with some friends, a ride in the car. We guarantee she'll have plenty of things to show you, too.

You already know that adopting a shelter dog means helping her overcome whatever abuse or neglect she may have endured, giving her the education she's been lacking, acting as the authority figure she's probably never had and shaping her into a worldly, responsible canine citizen. In this chapter, we'll suggest some creative ways for you to keep her mind and body occupied, to ease her adjustment into the world (and allow the world to adjust to *her!*) and to form a healthy, strong, lasting bond between you.

As they say, this could be the start of a beautiful friendship.

Different Dogs, Different Challenges

Of course, every adopted dog comes with her own set of personality quirks—good ones and bad ones. Your pup probably has some characteristics that make you beam and some that make you groan. But there are a few traits that surface repeatedly in adopted dogs that you'll need

Terrier mix Harry-O is out of the shelter and ready to face the world.

to be aware of and address. In the next sections, we've outlined some of the most common kinds of shelter dogs, but don't feel that you have to pigeonhole your pup into one of these profiles; she may not fit any of the descriptions, or she may fit more than one.

The Submissive Dog

Remember Carmen Brauchler from our introduction? When she was young, she was a classic submissive pup. She ducked when anyone reached toward her; she rolled over onto her back when anyone spoke firmly to her, and she generally didn't think very highly of herself. She felt like the low dog on the totem pole, and her family had to be patient and loving in order to build her confidence.

A submissive dog uses her body language to let everyone around her know how deferent she is. She may crouch or roll over on her back with her belly exposed when someone approaches, and she may piddle on the floor when someone leans over her or praises her. When she walks with or toward you, she may slink rather than prancing proudly. You'll often see her ears pressed back against her head and her tail between her legs. She tries hard not to call much attention to herself, and it's clear that she's low on self-confidence.

If your dog's a submissive type, you'll need to let her know that you think she's terrific and strong and important, even if she doesn't yet believe that herself. You'll have to be gentle when you train her or correct her for wrongdoing, and you mustn't let anyone make challenging moves toward her or yell at her. She'll benefit from lots of encouraging, non-threatening games and activities and a training class with lots of positive reinforcement and no harsh physical corrections. And you'll want to take her to new places and let her meet as many friendly people as possible—people who will approach her slowly, crouch down to her level to pet her and talk to her sweetly and happily.

Submissive dogs often avoid looking directly at people, so when you're alone, encourage her to make eye contact with you: hold her head in your hands gently and speak kindly to her until she looks at you. Then smile at her and tell her what a brave, wonderful pup she is. She needs to know that she can trust you—that you're her leader, but that you're never going to abuse her respect for you—and making eye contact is a good way to communicate that.

What she *doesn't* need is to be coddled. Don't correct her for things like rolling over or piddling on the floor when she feels particularly submissive, but don't reward her for them, either. And don't be *too* low-key and meek with her, since that may just reinforce her timidity. Your best bet is to play and talk with her in a happy, jolly, self-assured manner. Convey the sort of attitude you want her to have, and she'll learn from your example.

The Worried Dog

Worriedness and submissiveness often overlap, but they don't have to. The worried dog is a pup who frets over every loud noise, every strange-looking object, every unfamiliar person or situation. Dogs who grow up without loving, reassuring families—especially during early puppyhood—are likely to become worriers, so shelters are full

With love, knowledge and understanding, you can overcome just about any behavior problem.

of overly concerned canines. Sebastian Rubenstein was one of these: he spent his first few weeks shrinking in terror from all sorts of things, from ballpoint pens to remote controls to men with beards. He still has doubts about vacuum cleaners and exhaust fans, but he's learned to keep his anxiety in check, and he no longer fears new objects, experiences or people (even bearded ones).

Sebastian just needed to be exposed to as many new things and people as possible and to learn that they weren't going to hurt him. If your adopted dog is a worrier, the best thing you can do for her is *not* to shelter her from the things that frighten her. That doesn't mean, of course, that you should deliberately scare her, but you should make sure that she's introduced to new objects, noises and acquaintances every day.

If your dog is uncertain, for instance, about your remote control, let her get used to it slowly; show it to her (just put it down or hold it still in front of her; don't wave it in her face) and pet her. Say "What a brave girl . . . this remote control isn't scary!" or something similarly reassuring, and (as with a submissive dog) demonstrate to her that *you* are happy and confident in the presence of the remote control, so she can be too. You can do the same thing if she gets anxious about a thunderstorm or a plane flying overheard. But if she runs to you for salvation when she's scared by something, don't reward her timidity by cuddling and praising her; just be upbeat and try to take her mind off her fear by playing a game or having a training session.

When you introduce her to new people, follow the same procedure as with a submissive dog: Both you and the new person must make the encounter as casual, non-threatening, and cheerful as possible for your pup. Chatter with her, make eye contact with her, pet her, even have the new person slip her a treat if necessary. She'll learn that you're not going to put her in situations that will harm her, and gradually she'll begin to be a bit less on-edge about life in general.

By the way, lots of people who adopt submissive or shy dogs assume that their pups must have been physically abused in the past, and they respond with pity rather than positive training. More often than not, submission and shyness are the result not of direct abuse but of a lack of early education and socialization. If your dog cringes when you reach out to her, that doesn't necessarily mean she's been hit; more likely, it simply means she didn't grow up knowing that a hand moving toward her was something to welcome rather than fear. You can change her mind—but with gentle perseverance, not pity.

The Dominant Dog

If the submissive dog thinks she's the lowliest creature in the pack, the dominant dog thinks she's the alpha wolf, president, and pope all in one. She figures she could do just as good a job of ruling the roost as you, and she'd like to give it a try. Dominance surfaces in lots of big and small ways—from grabbing the leash out of your hands during a walk to guarding toys and furniture to biting another dog or person—and it can start small and become a big problem in a hurry. Lots of dogs show signs of dominance, especially during their teenaged years, when they're testing their limits and trying to figure out exactly where they fit in the family pack (remember, most dogs will assume just as much authority as they can get away with). And shelter dogs, who have often grown up without having to answer to anyone, are particularly prone to bossiness. If you feel as though your dog is starting to run your household, you need to waste no time in establishing and enforcing a pecking order.

The body language of a dominant dog conveys self-esteem in the extreme. She holds her head high, puts her ears up and forward and holds her ground when approached. When she feels threatened by a person or another dog, she raises her hackles and stands tall and proud. Whereas the submissive dog likes to take up as little space as possible, the dominant dog likes to make herself look as large as she can.

If you have a dominant puppy, you can help prevent her from becoming a dominant dog by doing a few simple exercises every day. Remember the exercises you used to test your puppy at the shelter, when you held her in the air and laid her on her side on the ground? You can use those same positions now to reassert your authority. Do them two or three times a day, and use them any time your pup gets bossy; if she squirms, talks back or tries to nip, give her a little shake and a sharp "ah-ah!" Then praise her when she's quiet and still, and don't release her until she's stopped wrestling with you.

You already know that obedience training will help you earn and keep your dog's respect, so signing up for a class is the first thing to do. Around the house, you need to show her in all sorts of little ways that she's not the top dog. Keep her umbilical-corded to you as much as possible in the beginning, since that's a kind and passive way to force her to follow you and let your actions govern hers. Insist that she sit for you before you give her treats or take her outside. Don't wrestle or play rough games (like tug-of-war) with her, and don't let her get on the furniture or sleep on your bed until she's learned beyond any doubt

Exercise, lots of exercise, is what active dogs like Sam need most.

who's in charge. And when you go for walks, be firm about not letting her drag you around or jump or lunge at people or dogs you meet. In short, convince *yourself* that you're the leader, and then convince *her.*

The Hyperactive Dog

This is the dog who can't sit still. She's always pacing, running in circles, pawing and bumping people for attention, getting into things, or whining to herself. She makes herself enough of a nuisance that, more often than not, she gets banished to her crate or the basement, where she just gets more agitated and hyper.

Hyperactivity usually results from a combination of boredom and nerves. Pacing and circling and whining may have become some of your dog's favorite pastimes when she was in a cage at the shelter; now, the stress of her new living situation may bring back these old habits with a vengeance. Needless to say, cooping her up isn't the answer. Regular exercise will help; it'll tire out her muscles and set her mind at ease. Training will help, not only because it will occupy her body and mind and give her new confidence, but also because she'll learn to do a sit-stay and down-stay that you can use when she gets too worked up. And since a lot of hyperactivity is dominance in disguise, it'll help put you back in control.

If your dog drives you crazy by being busy all the time, the two of you will have to compromise: You'll have to agree to give her more exercise, and she'll have to learn how to control her frenzies. Find some activities that you can enjoy together, and you'll both come to appreciate, rather than dread, her excess energy!

You'll find that with persistence and patience, you'll almost certainly be able to work through these problems. But what if your dog's behavior really gets out of hand? What if, despite your efforts, her dominance or spookiness or hyperactivity is making her hard to live with and doesn't seem to be improving? First, ask yourself honestly whether you've done everything possible to address the difficulty on your own. Second, third, and fourth, consult your veterinarian, the staff of the shelter where you adopted her and your obedience instructor. Since some behavior problems are caused by physical illness or discomfort, your vet can check to see whether your dog's troubles have a medical source. The shelter staff, who knew your dog before you did, may be able to give you some insights or suggestions about her behavior. And your instructor can work with you one-on-one to help remedy the situation, or refer you to another trainer who can.

Please don't give up on your dog. Don't even let yourself entertain the thought that she might be "hopeless," or she'll most likely sense your attitude and give up on you, too. It's very rare that a behavior problem is serious enough to require returning a dog to a shelter, and even if you believe you and your dog may have reached that point, that's *not* a decision you can or should make by yourself. If your vet, your instructor and the shelter staff feel that the match between you and your dog is destined to fail, then you may have no choice but to take her back. But you owe it to your dog to give her every chance. And you owe it to yourself, too, because you need to know that you've done everything possible for your dog, or you may feel guilty about having to give her up.

That's a worst-case scenario, of course, and while a lot of dogs *do* find themselves returned to the facilities from which they were adopted, very few of them actually have problems that couldn't be corrected with some time and work. So don't be worried about your dog's traits and habits; just set about turning her into the happy, well-rounded, well-adjusted dog she deserves to be. You two are going to have a great time, and your relationship will be all the stronger for the challenges you've faced together.

Spaying and Neutering

Before you and your new pup start sharing all kinds of great activities, it's important that she have all her vaccinations and that she be spayed or neutered if she's old enough. Living on the outside means being a responsible canine-and-human team, and that means protecting your dog's health and preventing her from contributing to the problem of dog overpopulation. So if your dog's not already spayed or neutered, please don't forget how crucial it is to have this procedure done as soon as possible. Your adoption contract probably gives you a time limit, but even if not, it's to your advantage—and to your dog's advantage—not to wait around.

If you've read this far, you're already well aware of the ethical and social issues that mandate spaying or neutering. Remember all those pups and dogs at the shelter? They were there because too many people let their dogs mate and have puppies—puppies for whom there weren't enough homes in the world. You and your dog certainly don't want to make the situation even worse.

But spaying or neutering will pay dividends closer to home, too. For a handful of reasons, altered dogs generally live longer and healthier lives than their unaltered counterparts. Their decreased hormonal drive makes them less apt to roam away from home in search of other dogs, so they're less likely to get lost, stolen or killed by cars or other animals or people.

Spaying and neutering offers more direct health benefits, too. For one thing, altered dogs are less likely to develop canine diabetes. Females are less prone to internal infections, and they're practically immune from mammary cancer, as are males from testicular cancer or prostate trouble.

You'll find your dog easier to live with after surgery. Males, in particular, tend to become less dominant and aggressive, and they often lose (or never develop) the urge to mark their territory with urine. Males and females alike are less inclined to embarrass you by mounting people or other dogs. Females won't go into heat twice a year, and that will spare you clean-up and the attention of the amorous male dogs in your neighborhood.

Does spaying or neutering make a dog fat or lazy? Nope. Too much food and too little exercise make a dog fat and lazy. That's the truth, and don't let anyone tell you otherwise.

Don't waste time feeling guilty for depriving your dog of a sex life. Remember, you're relieving her of her sex *drive,* and she's not going to miss what she doesn't want in the first place! She's going to be much more unhappy if she lives her whole life feeling sexually frustrated. And, by the way, having your dog altered doesn't reflect upon your own manliness or womanliness in the least—so uncross your legs and read on!

When you make an appointment for your dog's surgery, the vet's office will probably tell you to withhold food and possibly water for at least twelve hours before the surgery, and they may want your pup to spend the night at the office afterwards. The procedure involves the removal of the ovaries and uterus in females, and the removal of the testicles in males. Your dog will be under general anesthesia and won't feel a thing. A male dog will generally be up and around and feeling fine within a day after neutering; spaying a female is a bit more complicated, but she should be back to her old self within a couple days.

Although you'll want to keep an eye on your dog for a few days after the operation, you should know that complications are uncommon. Just follow the vet's instructions and keep your dog somewhat quiet; check her stitches to make sure they stay clean and unin-fected, and watch her so that she doesn't tear them out or bite or scratch at them. The vet will tell you when to come back to have the stitches removed (don't forget!), and that's the end of it.

Stepping Out

You don't have to conquer the world right away, but you can at least start giving your dog a taste of it. She's been living in a kennel for some time, and heaven only knows where she was before that, but now you can show her what it's like to live on the outside with you as her guide and protector. Whether she's dominant, submissive, hyperactive, shy or none of the above, she needs lots of exposure, exercise and encouragement if she's going to become (or remain) a confident, respectful,

Everyday experiences for you may be new ones for your adopted dog. Include her in as much of your life as possible, and she'll quickly get used to your ways.

happy dog. The more outings and experiences your dog has right from the beginning, the better adjusted she's going to be, period.

It's important for her to have her vaccinations immediately, by the way, since it's not safe for her to venture out before she's inoculated. Canine diseases are easily transmitted through contact and through the air, so be certain you've got your vet's okay before you take your dog to all sorts of exciting places with you.

Close to Home

Take your pup out on her leash, and give her a tour of your neighborhood. If she's never lived with a family before—or even if she has—she may not know about mailboxes, lamp posts, cars, cats. Don't let her roam unleashed even if you're watching her, since she probably doesn't know about avoiding trucks and not chasing other animals, and she may not know how to find her way home if she gets separated from you. That leash is your security, and when you and your dog are walking, there's simply no good reason not to use it.

Be courteous and friendly to the other people you encounter on your walks, and above all, respect their space. Don't let your dog run up to them, sniff them, lick them, bark at them or, worse, jump or lunge at them. But if they want to pet her, do have her sit and accept their praise. (When your dog is trained, you'll be able to use your sit-stay or down-stay to keep her calm and in place in the presence of new people, whether she's being petted or not.) If your dog is a dominant or hyper type, you may have to use your leash (a snap to the ground) and voice (an "Ah-ah" or "Easy!") to keep your dog from leaping up to bump or kiss the lucky stranger. If you've got a shy or submissive pup, you'll have to make the meeting as non-threatening as you can; ask the other person to crouch down and not make any quick moves or sudden noises. If the other person is a child, be sure that he or she knows better than to grab at your dog's ears or tail or put a small hand in her mouth. Above all, it's important that your dog's experiences with new people be good ones, and you're the one who's in charge of that.

Suppose you discover that your dog is afraid of certain kinds of people. You've already read about Ripple, who didn't trust children, and Sebastian, who wanted nothing to do with men with facial hair. Your dog may have similar fears; perhaps she doesn't like women, or older people or people wearing hats. There may be an easily identifiable reason for that (you may know, for example, that her previous owner had a beard and treated her unkindly). Chances are, though, you'll never be entirely certain of what caused her phobia, and what matters most is that you cure it. Don't avoid the kinds of people who scare your dog; seek them out, and create some positive experiences with them.

It's best not to encourage contact between your dog and other dogs on the street, even dogs who are accompanied by people and on-leash, unless you know the person and the dog and can be assured that the dog is healthy and friendly. Avoid unattached dogs, especially if you don't recognize them; just cross the street when you see one coming. And if your dog tries to go after a dog or other animal she spots, give her a snap on the leash and an "Ah-ah" to get her mind back where it belongs!

You do, however, want your dog to enjoy and get accustomed to the company of other pups; after all, she deserves a chance to pal around with members of her own species now and then. Obedience class, of course, is a great place for her to get used to other dogs, but you can probably find a friend or neighbor with a dog who'd be willing to take regular walks or trips to the park with you. (Again, it's wise to introduce the dogs on neutral ground in order to discourage territorial "border wars.") Let them play on-leash and then off-leash, in an enclosed area if possible.

One last reminder: Don't forget to take a pooper scooper or (more conveniently) a supply of plastic bags with you when you walk with your dog, since you'll have to clean up after her if she relieves herself. It's easy to do: Just slip a bag over your hand like a glove, pick up the mess, turn the bag inside out around it, and pitch it in the nearest trash can. You can be a neat and considerate dog walker without even getting your hands dirty. Unscooped poop not only spreads germs, but it's also a quick way to make your neighbors and other pedestrians dislike you, your dog and dogs in general. So please, for the sake of

Rottweilers Abby and Brenna enjoy each other's canine company.

Bright lights, big city, tiny puppy ripe for adventure!

all the other dogs and people who will walk where you walk, *do it!*

The Cosmopolitan Canine

Even if you live in a place with more gridlock than grass, where asphalt and skyscrapers are the rule, there's plenty to keep you and your dog entertained. The big city can be scary to an adopted dog, but it's also a great place for her to get used to some of the wildest sights, sounds and smells known to humans or dogs!

Since city sidewalks are often full of fast-moving people, it's extremely important for your urban dog to be able to walk on-leash at your side without straying or bothering anyone. She also needs to know that it's not all right to pick up litter or lick up spills from the pavement. When walking through a city crowd, keep your dog on a short (not tight) leash; you can even buy special one- or two-foot leashes, called *walking leashes* or *traffic handles*, for this purpose.

If your dog is worried about the strange things she encounters on city streets—from traffic noise to scaffolding to magazine vendors—don't avoid them (you probably couldn't if you tried!), but keep your attitude happy and reassuring and let her know she doesn't need to worry.

In the city as in the suburbs, it's your responsibility to clean up after your pup on your walks. Your city may have strict laws about dog waste and steep fines for not complying, but perhaps the best reason to tidy up is to help keep people-dog relations in your area as peaceful as they can be. Inconsiderate dog owners have prompted some cities to ban dogs altogether in certain areas. Don't let that happen to your hometown!

Dogs usually like window-shopping (and they're good at it, since they don't ask you to go inside and buy them things). Some stores may allow your dog inside, but that's a privilege reserved for trained dogs. Don't risk breaking merchandise or irritating shopkeepers or customers by taking a rowdy dog shopping with you. Your dog must know how to heel and do a sit-stay before she can hit the sales with you. And please don't leave your dog tied outside while *you* go into a building, even if you think you'll only be gone a minute; she could wrap her leash around something and choke herself, get into a fight with another dog or be stolen or hurt by someone. You can take your dog with you to most large pet-supply stores, but be careful: She *must* be fully vaccinated (since some of the hundreds of other dogs who were there before her may not have been), and she needs to know how to walk nicely at your side without helping herself to her favorite treats and toys off the shelf!

It can be tough to get away from the people and the pavement and the noises of the city, and it may seem nearly impossible to find a place where your dog can run and play and be crazy. Check out the parks near you; they may have enclosed areas where your dog can spend some time off her leash. If you can't find a convenient place to let your dog off-leash, invest in a twenty-five- or thirty-foot-retractable leash that will allow her to stretch her legs by running around you while you stand still. Many big-city parks even have daily or weekly play groups for dogs, often in the morning or on weekends, and these are a great way for you and your pup to have a ball, work off some energy and make new friends, as long as your dog is fully vaccinated and not prone to dominance or aggression.

The Working Dog

If you're one of the lucky people whose office or school allows dogs, why not take your new friend to work or class with you? Our dogs have all come to work with us, and we know lots of teachers, executives, and shopkeepers whose pups are regular fixtures at their workplaces.

Again, training is an absolute prerequisite. Nothing is more annoying to customers, coworkers or classmates than a disruptive dog, and if you work in a place where people will be coming in and out, you'll have to be sure that your dog is friendly to strangers and won't try to run out the door.

Don't take your dog to work or school unless you're completely certain that her presence will be welcomed and her behavior will be stellar. But if it is an option, she'll love being with you all day, and you'll love having her there!

Games and Sports

It may sound odd, but a lot of shelter dogs don't know how to play. If your dog hasn't grown up with human and canine playmates, she may not understand the concept of games, and you'll need to teach her a few things about having fun. On the other hand, if she's an old hat at game-playing, then she'll probably be able to show *you* a few good tricks. (There are some dogs who just aren't amused by games, and that's all right, too.)

Doggie games don't have to be original to be entertaining. Fetch is an all-time favorite, though it too often turns from "fetch" into "throw a toy, watch your dog pick it up and run away with it, and chase after her until you get frustrated," which is short-lived and not terribly much fun! You can teach your dog that returning with her toy is half the fun of fetching if you keep her *on-leash* to start. Pick a toy or ball that your dog really loves, and get her interested in it; then toss it a few feet away and say "Fetch!" or "Get it!" in an excited voice. Encourage her to pick up the toy, and when she does, tell her she's a good girl and encourage her to bring it back to you by calling her, pulling lightly on her leash, and backing away from her and clapping your hands. When she gets to you, get the toy out of her mouth by squeezing the sides of her snout, removing the object, and saying "Out" or "Give." Then *praise* her like crazy, and do it again. This way, she'll learn that only by bringing the toy or ball back to you can she earn your praise and keep the game going. When she's got the hang of it, try taking her off her leash, but if she fetches her toy and takes off, refuse to give chase, and put her back on-leash next time.

If simple fetching is too elementary for your talented pup, try hiding the toy or ball and sending her to find it. Your dog can learn to distinguish among her toys if you give each toy a distinct name ("ball," "rope bone," "pink rubber porcupine"), and she'll probably enjoy the challenge of being told to find and fetch a certain plaything.

Try playing hide-and-seek with your dog, too. Encouraging her to come and find you by using her eyes and nose will strengthen the connection between you even more—especially if you always go wild with praise when she locates you.

Don't play games like wrestling and tug-of-war, which pit you against your dog in a battle of strength and will. To us, these are just friendly contests, but to a dog, they're serious challenges. Particularly if your dog has dominant tendencies, you mustn't encourage her to growl at you and challenge your authority during playtime, or she may decide that it's all right to do so at other times, too. At no time should she put her teeth on you during play, either. If, for example, she snaps at your hands when you're holding her retrieving toy—even if it's an accident—give her a nipping correction and decrease your rowdiness level.

Lots of dogs who enjoy fetching also enjoy playing Frisbee, but please be careful: dogs who leap into the air and twist their bodies to catch Frisbees may look impressive, but they're at an extraordinarily high risk for injury. We've known dogs who became paralyzed after sustaining spinal injuries during Frisbee games. So resist the urge to throw your Frisbee above your dog's eye level, and don't encourage or allow her to jump and twist to catch it.

Backyard games are a blast, but don't forget to venture into the great outdoors with your new pup as well: exercise does wonders for the body and mind—yours as well as your dog's. If you're an athletic, outdoorsy type, your new pup will probably be more than happy to join you in your activities. And if you're traditionally more of an armchair athlete, then maybe she'll give you the incentive you need to get out and get moving!

For dogs as for people, a thorough checkup is advisable before you start any sort of serious exercise regimen. And you'll want to keep an eye on her at all times for any signs of muscle strain, foreign objects in her eyes or feet, heat exhaustion and burned paws in warm weather, and frozen paws in cold weather. Check her for ticks, burrs, or cut pads on her paws after every workout. Don't forget to give her plenty of water when she's exercising, and keep in mind that the temperature outdoors will have a greater effect on her than it will on you, since she can't change clothes like you can! Woolly dogs shouldn't overexert themselves in hot weather, and small, short-coated breeds (who can't regulate their body temperatures as effectively as larger dogs) may need a sweater to keep them cozy in winter. Finally, please don't

Bill and Golden Retriever Katahdin are mountain-climbing buddies; Katahdin even carries his share of the gear.

immediately try to run the Boston Marathon or swim the English Channel with your pup; she, like you, will have to work up to her athletic goals slowly!

Do you jog? Why not let your dog be your running buddy? It's a pleasure to jog with a dog who knows how to stay with you on her leash. Start by taking her on very short jaunts with you, and if she seems to enjoy herself, add to your distance until you know just how far and how fast she can comfortably go. Don't forget to take her water bottle with you and to watch her carefully for signs of fatigue or distress. (Healthy, rugged dogs can make great hikers, too!)

You can also train your dog to run with you as you bike, if you take the time to get her accustomed to the oddities of two-wheelers. Again, she needs to know how to walk and jog on a leash first, since she could cause a serious accident or get seriously hurt by running between your wheels or cutting in front of you. Start by walking your bicycle at your right side and your dog at your left side. (If she's worried about the bike, let her approach and sniff it while it's stationary first.) Then put the bike between you and your dog as you walk. If she gets too close to the wheels, give her a sharp leash snap away from them. When she's

Ava's in her life jacket and ready for a swim.

trotting happily beside you and not interfering with the movement of the bicycle, you can begin to take short, slow rides with her, and gradually increase your distance and speed.

If you live near a lake or beach that allows dogs (or if you have a pool and don't mind a little dog hair floating in it!), you and your dog might enjoy swimming together. Some dogs—especially Retrievers, Spaniels, and other water dogs or mixes of water dogs—take naturally to the water, while others may be more hesitant. If your dog is worried at first, wade with her into some shallow water, and throw a floating toy or stick if necessary to encourage her to start dog-paddling. It's important to watch her carefully, even if she's a strong, experienced swimmer, and it's a good idea to keep her on a long rope (but not your retractable leash) so that she can't swim out of your reach.

Don't force swimming on a reluctant pup. And *please* don't throw her in the water in an attempt to teach her to swim. If, after a few trips to the lake or the beach, she still isn't keen on swimming, don't push it. (You may find that some dogs love the water but just aren't built for swimming—like Ava, whose stocky terrier body didn't seem to want to stay afloat. But now she's outfitted with a special doggie life vest, and she's practically a canine Mark Spitz.)

One last activity that's become a favorite of thousands of dogs and people in the last few years is a neat sport called agility. There are probably at least a few agility clubs or training clubs with agility courses in your area. An agility course is a canine obstacle course, with ramps and seesaws and hoops and jumps for the dogs to navigate while their people run alongside them. The obstacles aren't dangerous, but they require sure footing, concentration, and confidence, so many training schools and clubs offer agility classes in which you can teach your dog (using positive reinforcement only, never force) to negotiate the obstacles and have a ton of fun at the same time. Some organizations hold agility trials, in which teams compete for prizes according to their speed and accuracy, but lots of people take agility classes just for the sake of getting the exercise and boosting their dogs' physical and mental confidence. We strongly encourage you to enroll yourself and your new pup in a good agility class (basic obedience training may be a prerequisite). It's tough to find a better all-around activity for dogs whose brains and bodies need exercise and entertainment.

The Canine Good Citizen Test

In 1989 the American Kennel Club established a program to test and reward conscientious dogs and their people. The non-competitive Canine Good Citizen (CGC) test awards certificates and CGC titles to dog-human teams who demonstrate their responsibility and training. In coming years, CGC titles may even be able to earn special privileges and benefits for dogs who hold them; for example, Canine Good Citizens may be able to stay in hotels where non-certified dogs aren't allowed.

CGC tests are often sponsored by training clubs and kennel clubs, either in conjunction with or separately from obedience trials or dog shows; your instructor or vet can probably tell you about upcoming tests. The tests themselves are much less formal than obedience trials. For starters, they're open to all dogs, regardless of breeding or registration. The scoring is all pass/fail, and the evaluators are looking only for basic good behavior and temperamental soundness, not precision and perfection. You can generally give as many commands as you need to get your dog to do what she's supposed to (though you, of course, will have trained her to respond to you on the *first* command!). And you only have to pass the test once in order to get your title and certificate.

All the exercises on the test are ones you can expect to cover in a good basic obedience class. But if you're interested in earning a CGC title, ask your instructor for some extra help and practice on the specific activities you'll need to perform. Some obedience schools and clubs offer special Canine Good Citizen classes, designed especially for people and dogs pursuing the CGC. A dog who's completed basic training and is confident without being shy or overbearing is a perfect candidate for a CGC title.

When you enter your dog in a CGC test, you'll be scored on the following items:

- *Appearance and grooming.* The evaluator will check your dog for cleanliness and good health, and will handle and brush her lightly.

- *Accepting a stranger.* The evaluator will approach you, shake your hand, and speak to you, and your dog must not jump at him or shy away. (In this as in other exercises, you can give a "stay" command to remind your dog to stay put.)

- *Walking on a loose lead.* You and your dog will be asked to walk together on a loose lead and make several turns and halts. (A dog who understands "let's go" or "heel" will do just fine.)

- *Walking through a crowd.* You'll walk your dog on-leash past several unfamiliar people, and she won't be allowed to run up to them or bother them.

- *Sitting for examination.* Your dog will sit at your left side without jumping up or shying away while the evaluator pets her.

- *Sitting and lying down on command.* Simple enough: You'll have your dog on-leash and will be asked to make her sit and lie down on command.

- *Staying in position.* You'll leave your dog in a sit-stay or a down-stay and walk about twenty feet away; your dog won't be allowed to move until the evaluator tells you to release her.

- *Reaction to another dog.* You and your dog will approach another dog-person team, and you'll shake hands with the other person. The dogs won't be allowed to approach each other (again, you can give a "stay" command if you wish).

- *Reaction to distractions.* Your dog will be tested on her reaction to various unusual noises or sights, like a dropped book or a person with a shopping cart or on crutches. She's allowed to be startled and move around as long as she doesn't panic or lose control.

- *Being left alone.* You'll leave your dog on a long leash with the evaluator while you go out of sight for a few minutes. She doesn't have to stay (although you may tell her to if you wish), but she can't pace, whine, or cause trouble.

Again, precision isn't what counts at a CGC test; what matters is that you and your dog prove that you're the sort of dog-human team that other dogs and humans can enjoy being around. As you can see, these are the kinds of exercises and situations you've already been exploring with your pup to get her used to the ways of the world. Practicing for a CGC test is a great incentive to keep exposing her to new people and new distractions, and a CGC certificate is a nice reward for all the good work you're doing with your new pup anyway!

Continuing Education

Nothing builds confidence and strengthens canine-human bonds like working and learning together, so advanced obedience work may be just the ticket for you and your adopted dog. The more you and your dog train together, the more you'll both enjoy it. Once you've got that first basic obedience class under your belts, your pup will have learned how to learn, and you'll have learned how to teach her. Once you've mastered the basic exercises, you can move on to more exciting and challenging ones.

Lots of dog obedience schools and virtually all dog training clubs offer advanced obedience classes. If you've enjoyed your basic training class, and your training school or club offers further classes, you're in luck; if not, call around again, just as you did when you first took your dog to school. Since upper-level training classes are usually ongoing courses (that is, you'll probably enroll for several eight- or ten-week sessions rather than just one), it's especially important to find an instructor with whom you and your dog are really comfortable, and, if possible, to visit an advanced class before you sign up. You'll probably discover that advanced classes are much more self-paced and usually more informal than introductory classes, and that the camaraderie among the students is something you'll want to be a part of!

The goal of most (but not all!) advanced students is, eventually, to show their dogs in obedience trials and earn obedience titles. Not so long ago, obedience was a sport for purebreds only, but now mixed breeds can join in the fun as well. No matter what your dog is, though, she'll have to be registered with at least one dog registry organization if you intend to show her. In order to earn obedience titles from the American Kennel Club, your dog must be a purebred of a breed recognized by the AKC, and you'll need to provide proof of her ancestry *or* file for an Indefinite Listing Privilege (ILP) if she, like most shelter or breed rescue purebreds, is of uncertain heritage.

Mixed-breed dogs can be registered with the Mixed Breed Dog Club of America, which sponsors more and more obedience trials every year and awards titles that correspond to the AKC obedience titles. If your dog is a mixed breed (or a purebred, too), you can register and show her through the United Kennel Club. UKC obedience trials are slightly different from AKC and MBDCA trials, but most of the exercises are basically the same. A dog can earn titles from more than one organization. Appendix C lists the addresses of these three registries; write to them and request information on registering your dog and showing her in obedience trials.

The nice thing about obedience trials is that they're competitive and non-competitive at the same time. When you and your dog enter an obedience trial, you'll be in a class with probably three to fifty other dogs and handlers. When your number is called, you'll go into the "ring" (which will actually be rectangular) and perform a set of prescribed exercises for a judge, who will give you a score from zero to 200 points, with 170 as the cutoff between passing and failing. If your score is among the four highest in the class, you'll get a ribbon and maybe a trophy or other prize, but as long as you get at least 170 points and complete all the exercises satisfactorily, you'll earn a "leg" toward your obedience title, whether or not you outscore anyone else in the class. When you and your dog receive three passing scores, you've got yourselves an obedience title and a certificate to go with it. You can be a rousing success without ever "defeating" another team.

Go to an obedience trial as a spectator if you want to learn more about showing your dog (leave her at home, though, since unentered dogs aren't allowed at dog shows). Your training school or club can tell you when and where upcoming trials will be held. Trials are lots of fun, and you'll be impressed by the dogs and handlers you see, but beware: Some beginners get intimidated and scared off by watching the advanced dogs compete and feeling certain that they and *their* dogs could never stack up. Just remember that the dogs at an obedience trial aren't little robots; they're regular, happy, funny, mischievous dogs just like yours. And their performance and teamwork is the result of a lot of hard work. Your dog can do every bit as well. And don't let anyone tell you that you *have* to start with a specially bred puppy in order to do well in obedience. In fact, in the last few years, some of the most prestigious obedience competitions in the nation have been won by dogs adopted from shelters at five or six years of age.

There are three levels of competitive obedience, each more difficult (and, we think, more fun) than the last, and three titles you can earn:

- *Novice.* This is the first step, the class in which you and your dog will have to show your proficiency at heeling on- and off-leash, standing and staying on command, coming when called and sitting or lying down and staying in a line of other dogs (you and the other handlers will stand at the other side of the ring). Do it all well three times, and you've earned a Companion Dog title and the right to put the letters CD (or, in the case of a United Kennel Club title, U-CD) after your dog's name.

- *Open.* The Open class requires your dog to be even more athletic and independent than in the Novice class. Here, your dog will have to heel off-leash, come when called and then lie down in mid-flight, retrieve a dumbbell on flat ground and over a high jump, clear a broad jump and perform a sit-stay and a down-stay

Alfy, CDX, who at age eleven still loves obedience work, sails over the broad jump at an obedience trial.

with the other dogs in the class while you and the other handlers leave the ring and go out of sight. (We hear you thinking "Oh, my dog could *never* do that!"—but you'd be amazed at all she can do!) Three passing scores in this class win you a Companion Dog Excellent title and the letters CDX or U-CDX after your pup's name.

- *Utility.* This is the decathlon of obedience trials. In the Utility class, dogs perform a variety of impressive exercises, including executing Novice class commands in response to hand signals only, using their noses to sniff out dumbbells touched by their handlers and leaping over different jumps according to their handlers' directions. It's tough stuff, and when you've accumulated your three passing scores, you and your dog will wear your Utility Dog (UD or U-UD) title with pride.

Whether you win, place or show, you and your dog will have a great time training for obedience trials if you both stay positive and don't forget that fun and education, not ribbons and prizes, are the real goal of advanced obedience work. When it ceases to be fun, that's when it's time to take a break, but otherwise, we think you'll find that higher education can be the source of lots of fun and learning.

Lending a Helping Paw

By this point, we hope, you're making your dog happy and she's making you happy. Why not take the next step and make some other people happy, too? Dogs are among the most therapeutic and diplomatic of all nature's critters, and once your pup is fully trained and fully adapted to her new life, maybe she can become an ambassador of canine goodwill.

It's been scientifically proven over and over (though dog lovers knew it all along) that dogs literally reduce blood pressure and stress levels in the people they're around. So hospitals, nursing homes, children's homes and other care and shelter facilities frequently invite Therapy Dogs to visit and cheer up their residents. Pet therapy, with its naturally soothing methods of stress relief, has come to be viewed by many as "the wave of the future," as one woman whose shelter pup has become a Therapy Dog told us.

Obviously, training is a must for any dog who will be interacting with old, young, infirm or wary people. She'll have to know how to heel, stay in various positions and come when called; and, if she knows any other exercises or tricks, those will be a nice bonus for her audience. Her manners will have to be impeccable so that she doesn't disturb, frighten or jostle anyone.

A Therapy Dog has to have a stable, calm temperament, too, so that the occasional stresses of therapy work won't upset her. She needs to be trusting of people, comfortable working around wheelchairs and walkers and medical equipment and unflappable in the face of people who may not immediately warm up to her or handle her gently, since many of the residents she'll visit may be physically impaired in some way or simply unused to interacting with dogs. And she needs to love her work, since a happy Therapy Dog is a successful Therapy Dog.

An organization called Therapy Dogs International certifies Therapy Dogs once they've demonstrated their competence; contact TDI (their address is in Appendix C) for more information on becoming a registered therapy team. Or ask your shelter or training school whether they have a therapy program. Some shelters even allow volunteers to take their puppies for visits to convalescent homes; if your shelter doesn't have a program like this, you could suggest starting one while you're teaching your own pup to be a full-fledged Therapy Dog.

As people involved in pet therapy will tell you, there's nothing quite as rewarding as sharing a little of your doggie love with people who really need it. And Therapy Dogs seem to agree.

Here's to a beautiful friendship!

Doing Nothing at All

There's no rule that says that you and your dog have to be moving at warp speed every moment of your lives. It's terrific to be active and be busy together, but it's also nice just to *be* together sometimes. Silence and touch and eye contact are means of communicating with your dog just as words and activities are. Set aside a few minutes each day to sit still with your dog, to look each other in the eyes and enjoy each other's company without needing to say or do anything.

So you've rescued your special dog or puppy; you've outfitted and educated her; you've given her the confidence and courtesy she needs to be content and make other people content. Congratulations on a job well-done! Sure, there will still be setbacks and annoyances, but they'll get less frequent and less important as you and your dog grow closer and understand each other better. You've got lots of good times ahead of you, full of learning and fun and love.

When things get rough, just remember a few things. First and foremost, there's plenty of help available. Let your obedience instructor, your vet and your shelter staff give you a hand if you get frustrated with your pup. She *wants* to be good, after all, and you simply need to find the best way to show her how.

Don't forget to keep exercising and educating your dog through-out her life. Idle canine bodies and minds are mischief waiting to happen. Activities and training are fun for *you*, too, and they'll keep the friendship between you and your pup growing stronger all the time.

And finally, remind yourself every now and then of what your dog was like when you first got her from the shelter, when she was probably some combination of scared, over-excited, uneducated and unloved. You've brought her a long way, and you both deserve a scratch behind the ears for that.

This is where we leave you. But it's not an end, of course; it's the start of many happy, happy years for you and your adopted pup.

APPENDIX A

Adoption Alternatives

Perhaps you've decided that you want a certain kind of dog that you can't seem to find in a shelter. Or maybe you just don't feel quite comfortable adopting from any of the shelters around you. That's okay; there are other ways to give a good home to a needy dog, like breed rescue societies and racing Greyhound rescue societies. It may take a little more innovation to find one of these, but they're becoming more popular and easier to locate all the time, and they can help match you up with a great pup.

Breed Rescue Societies

For practically every breed of dog, there is a national breed club with lots of local chapters. And in the last few years, many of those clubs have taken on the challenge of rescuing dogs of their chosen breed from shelters and pounds and placing them into secure adoptive homes. Now there are clubs devoted entirely to breed rescue, and if you're interested in adopting a purebred, they're a great resource.

Breed rescue societies rely on their volunteer members to rescue dogs from adoption facilities or from people who can't or shouldn't keep them. These volunteers, who are usually knowledgeable "dog people" who have experience with dog raising and training in general and the breed in particular, serve as foster parents to the dogs until permanent homes can be found. Ideally, they not only feed and groom and exercise the rescued dogs but also give them some socialization and basic education.

The foster-home system can translate into a big advantage for you when you adopt a dog through a breed rescue program, since your pup will have had at least some experience living in a household and learning rules by the time you get her. She'll probably have begun to get used to other dogs, too, since most breed rescue volunteers already have dogs of their own. And her "foster parents" will be able to tell you a lot about her personality and her needs, since they'll have lived with her day and night for some time. So it's important to adopt from a rescue society whose members you trust and whose foster parents know what they're doing.

You won't find a breed rescue society for every single breed of dog in your area; sometimes there's just not enough demand for one (after all, a Karelian Bear Dog Rescue Society in central Texas probably wouldn't be very busy), and sometimes there's not enough interest or person-power. But most areas will at least have rescue clubs for the breeds that appear most frequently in animal shelters—that is, the most popular breeds at any given time. (Remember, if you want a dog of a very popular breed, be *very* patient and judicious in your selection, since popularity usually leads to overbreeding, and overbreeding usually leads to dogs with temperamental and physical problems.)

Your veterinarian or a local training school may have a list of local breed rescue clubs and contacts for the breed or breeds you're seeking. Or they may be able to give you a list of local breed clubs; you can call them and ask whether they do any rescue work. If you can't find breed clubs near you, you can write to the American Kennel Club (see Appendix C for the address) and request a list. You can also order a directory of practically all the breed rescue clubs in the nation by contacting Project BREED (**B**reed **R**escue **E**fforts and **ED**ucation) and requesting a copy of their latest source book (see Appendix C for the address).

When you contact a specific breed rescue club, you'll find out exactly how they conduct their adoptions, whether you'll be asked to visit dogs at their foster homes or elsewhere, for instance, and what will be required of you before and after the adoption. Remember, rescue societies (especially those dealing with relatively uncommon breeds) don't have as many animals available for adoption at a given time as shelters do, so you may have to wait a while until the right dog comes along. But if you're patient and work with the club, chances are, you'll come away with a fantastic canine buddy.

Retired Racing Greyhound Adoption

More and more states are legalizing Greyhound racing every year. It seems to many citizens and legislators like a harmless and entertaining way to raise money, but the terrible, non-sugar-coatable truth is that it's a cruel exhibition responsible for the abuse and death of countless beautiful Greyhounds. Racing dogs aren't loved and valued pets; they're commodities, kept in kennels and given just as much care as it takes to keep them in running condition. When they're past their prime (usually by age five or so), they're generally euthanized (often by less-than-humane methods) or left to die. And the less-swift dogs who don't win at the tracks are even less fortunate: they're killed or abandoned even earlier in life.

Greyhound rescue groups have evolved to try make the best of a very, very bad situation. They place retired or non-winning racing dogs into adoptive homes in an attempt to make the later years of their lives more pleasant than the first few years. That still doesn't take the scourge out of Greyhound racing, of course, but as long as the "sport" is around, the rescue clubs are doing their best to reduce the damage it does.

Even though racing Greyhounds haven't lived in real homes before, they usually make gentle, loving pets, and they don't need any more socialization and education than any other adopted dogs. If you're interested in rescuing a racer, Cynthia Branigan's book, *Adopting the Racing Greyhound* (New York: Howell Book House, 1992; see Appendix C) will inform you about all aspects of the process. You can also contact the following organizations for information on finding, rescuing and raising a Greyhound:

REGAP
(**RE**tired **G**reyhounds **A**s **P**ets)
P.O. Box 41307
St. Petersburg, FL 33743
813/347-2206

Greyhound Pets of America
5 Carleton Avenue
Randolph, MA 02368
800/366-1472

Greyhound Friends, Inc.
167 Saddle Hill Road
Hopkinton, MA 01748
508/435-5969

Other Ways You Can Help

So now you've done a great job with *your* pup, and maybe, just maybe, you're inspired to help other homeless dogs as well Great! There are lots of ways you can keep making a difference no matter how much or how little of your time and money you can spare. Here are a few ideas for you:

Volunteer at a Shelter

There's no more direct way to help out than by volunteering your time at an animal shelter—and no better way to repay the shelter that gave you *your* dog than by giving it some of your time! Just about any adoption facility will welcome your help, though the duties you'll be asked to do may vary from shelter to shelter. There's always much to be done at a shelter: There are dogs to walk, cages to clean, dogs and cats to bathe and groom and feed and socialize and medications to administer. At small shelters, which may be run almost entirely by volunteers, you may even get to help by transporting animals to the vet, making house checks and eventually counseling potential adopters and filling out adoption paperwork.

Even if you don't feel that you're physically (or emotionally) able to work directly with the animals, you can still be a big help to a shelter. Adoption facilities—especially small ones without large office staffs— almost always need help with fundraising, and many can use extra hands and brains for publicity, paperwork, telephoning and newsletter publishing, too. If you have special talents—if you're a good artist or writer, for example—you may be able to put those skills to use.

The extent of the responsibilities a shelter will entrust to you will depend on a lot of things: how well-staffed and well-established the shelter is already, how much (if any) prior experience you've had with dogs and how long you've been volunteering. But most shelters will appreciate your hard work, your new ideas and your enthusiasm, as long as you're always respectful of the way the facility is managed.

Volunteering doesn't have to involve a large time commitment, though most shelters will ask that you work during the same time slot every week. An hour or two on Saturday afternoon isn't a big chunk out of your week, but it will mean the world to the shelter staff and to the dogs you can walk during that time! So call your favorite animal shelter and ask about specific volunteer opportunities, and you can become a terrific friend to lots of special dogs like yours.

Make a Donation to a Shelter or Humane Organization

Maybe you're short on time, but you still want to help. Shelters always need donations of money (in any amount!) and supplies. Most of them publish "wish lists" in their newsletters, or they'll be happy to tell you on the phone what specific items they need. Generally, supplies such as food, food bowls, leashes, collars, crates and toys are in demand, but always check first before you buy or bring such items to a shelter; you don't want to give them something they won't be able to use. Lots of shelters also need old newspapers to line their cages, and many collect old towels and blankets to use as bedding.

Shelters are always looking for larger items, too; their wish lists may include things such as fans, heaters, window air conditioners, refrigerators, photocopy machines and even used vans or trucks. Perhaps you or your company has one of these items around and would like to find a new home for it. Remember, your donation will probably be tax-deductible, and it'll make an enormous difference to many, many people and dogs!

Maybe you'd like to support one of the larger humane organizations in its efforts to control pet overpopulation, promote spaying and neutering and encourage responsible animal care. Appendix C lists the addresses and phone numbers of several organizations that work hard on behalf of animals and will be most grateful for your donation.

Become a Foster Parent

Shelters and breed rescue societies often need people to foster dogs in their homes until the dogs can find permanent homes. It's a big job, just like fostering a child, and it takes a good deal of time, energy, patience and strength. Don't consider becoming a doggie foster parent until you and your adopted dog have been together for a while, are secure and comfortable and aren't dealing with any major behavior or adjustment problems. And *definitely* don't attempt to become a foster family if your dog shows any dominant, aggressive or territorial tendencies; she needs a steady enough temperament that she won't mind having new dogs sharing her living space and your attention now and again.

Fostering a dog means keeping her in your home, feeding her, walking her and socializing her until she's adopted. That could mean a couple days, or it could mean several weeks. Sometimes it's a smooth process, and sometimes it's not: You may end up opening your home to a dog with some behavior troubles, so it will be helpful if you've had some training experience. Often, fostering a dog also means being available to show her to prospective adopters and answer their questions, and that may be a strain on your schedule.

Not all shelters use foster homes, but many do place their injured dogs, very young puppies, or badly abused or neglected animals into temporary homes with experienced "dog people" who know how to care for them. Some small shelters also place their "surplus" animals—those who are healthy and adoptable, but for whom there isn't any room at the adoption facility—into foster care. Call your local shelter to find out whether it has a foster program, and how you can get involved.

Breed rescue organizations, which usually don't have facilities of their own, rely heavily on foster homes. If you've got a favorite breed or two—preferably breeds with which you've had some experience in the past—see Appendix A for tips on finding a rescue group near you, and ask about foster opportunities.

You have probably already guessed the number-one danger in fostering dogs. That's right: You might fall in love with one and find that you can't bear to give her up. So if you're considering becoming a foster parent, either promise yourself at the outset that you're positively *not* going to keep any of the dogs you house, or be certain that you'll be able to accommodate another pup if you know you might be tempted to adopt one!

Spread the Word

You know now how happy an adopted dog can make you, and you know how sad life can be for those shelter dogs who aren't adopted. So don't keep your knowledge to yourself. If you have friends or family members who are thinking of adding dogs to their ranks, suggest adoption to them, and recommend a good shelter. If you discover that your neighbors are planning to breed their biting, bowlegged dog, talk to them about the problem of pet overpopulation, and refer them to a low-cost spay/neuter program. If you see someone who's getting angry because his or her dog is jumping or nipping, politely offer a few words of advice on solving the problem. Don't be shy about speaking to people about responsible dog care and education; we find that they usually appreciate the information!

And by all means, if you see or know of someone who's abusing or neglecting his or her dog, don't look the other way. Either approach the person yourself if you feel it's safe, or call your local authorities and report a case of animal cruelty.

Most shelters have flyers and posters available, and they'll be happy to have you take a stack and pass them around or post them. They'll probably even have holiday cards, address labels, shirts, hats, bags, dog supplies or other stuff that you can purchase to show your support.

You might want to speak to your local shelter about starting a humane-education program (or getting involved in an already-existing one): You could visit schools, day camps, or scout meetings with a well-behaved shelter dog (yours!) and talk about the right and wrong ways to treat animals. Tell them why it's important not to produce more puppies. Explain why it's not okay to chain, hit or tease a dog, and show them how docile and enjoyable your dog is when they're gentle and kind to her. Humane education is a rewarding and incredibly important undertaking, since teaching children to have compassion and respect for animals is probably our best chance to stem the tide of future cruelty and overpopulation.

Adopt Another Dog

Are two adopted dogs better than one? Well, very possibly! Once your adopted pup is all settled into your home, and you know that she's not an aggressive or overly dominant or jealous dog, you might just find yourself itching for another canine companion. There are, of course, pros and cons to that idea: Another dog will mean more money, more time, more housebreaking and training. But now that you've been through the process once, you'll probably find that the second time around is considerably less stressful for you.

And you may also find—after the initial adjustment period has passed—that in some ways it's actually *easier* to have two dogs than to have just one. Remember, dogs are pack animals; they're used to living in groups, and they usually like it. If you're careful to adopt a second dog whose personality won't clash with that of your first, and if you introduce them gently and without playing favorites, they can become great friends, entertain each other and keep each other from getting lonely and bored when you can't be home.

A second (or third or—dare we say it—fourth!) dog can bring both you and your adopted pup lots of pleasure, provided you're just as careful and conscientious about subsequent adoptions as you've been about the first one, and provided you don't bite off more than you can chew!

Strut Your Stuff!

Most importantly, show off your adopted dog! Don't keep her to yourself; take her places and introduce her to people. Make sure she's always neat, clean and courteous and kind to the people and dogs around her. Show everyone how sweet and civilized she is, and then tell them all that she's an adopted dog and a truly terrific companion!

APPENDIX C

Recommended Reading and Other Resources

An educated dog is a happy, responsible dog; and an educated dog lover is a happy, responsible dog lover! Here's a starter list of books, videotapes, magazines, hot lines and organizations that will help you and your dog get the most out of each other. (You should be able to find or order most of these books, tapes and magazines through a local bookstore or pet-supply store.)

Don't stop with these, of course. There are lots of great materials and resources available, and more appear every day. Scout them out, and make yourself the best-read dog person on your block!

Books

Benjamin, Carol Lea. *The Chosen Puppy: How to Select and Raise a Great Puppy from an Animal Shelter.* New York: Howell Book House, 1990.

—. *Dog Problems.* New York: Howell Book House, 1989.

—. *Second-Hand Dog: How to Turn Yours into a First-Rate Pet.* New York: Howell Book House, 1988.

—. *Surviving Your Dog's Adolescence: A Positive Training Program.* New York: Howell Book House, 1993.

Branigan, Cynthia. *Adopting the Racing Greyhound.* New York: Howell Book House, 1992.

Carlson, Delbert G., and James M. Giffin. *The Dog Owner's Home Veterinary Handbook.* New York: Howell Book House, 1992.

Davis, Kathy Diamond. *Responsible Dog Ownership.* New York: Howell Book House, 1994.

—. *Therapy Dogs: Training Your Dog to Reach Others.* New York: Howell Book House, 1992.

Evans, Job Michael. *The Evans Guide for Civilized City Canines*. New York: Howell Book House, 1990.

—. *The Evans Guide for Housetraining Your Dog*. New York: Howell Book House, 1987.

—. *People, Pooches, and Problems*. New York: Howell Book House, 1991.

Kilcommons, Brian. *Good Owners, Great Dogs*. New York: Warner Books, 1992.

McLennan, Bardi. *Dogs and Kids: A Guide for Parents*. New York: Howell Book House, 1993.

Milan, Ellie. *Two Hundred Ways to Enjoy Your Dog*. Loveland: Alpine, 1990.

The Monks of New Skete. *How to Be Your Dog's Best Friend: A Training Manual for Dog Owners*. Boston: Little, Brown, and Co., 1978.

Randolph, Mary. *Dog Law*. Berkeley: Nolo Press, 1988.

Siegal, Mordecai, and Matthew Margolis. *When Good Dogs Do Bad Things*. Boston: Little, Brown, and Co., 1986.

Tortora, Daniel. *The Right Dog for You: Choosing a Breed that Matches Your Personality, Family, and Lifestyle*. New York: Fireside, 1983.

Volhard, Jack and Wendy. *The Canine Good Citizen: Every Dog Can Be One*. New York: Howell Book House, 1994.

Volhard, Jack, and Gail Fisher. *Training Your Dog the Step-by-Step Way*. New York: Howell Book House, 1987.

Walkowicz, Chris, and Bonnie Wilcox. *Old Dogs, Old Friends*. New York: Howell Book House, 1991.

Magazines

Shelter Sense (publication of the Humane Society of the United States)
2100 L Street NW
Washington, DC 20037
202/452-1100

Dog Fancy
Fancy Publications
P.O. Box 6040
Mission Viejo, CA 92690
714/855-8822

Hot Lines

Animal Poison Hotline at the University of Illinois
217/333-3611

800 for Animals, Inc. Animal Information Line (provides referrals and information on canine services and organizations)
800/8-ANIMAL (800/826-4625)

Friends of Animals, Inc. (low-cost spay/neuter program referral)
800/631-2212
Human–Animal Program's Pet Loss Support Hotline
916/752-4200

Humane Organizations

**The American Humane
Association**
63 Inverness Drive East
Englewood, CO 80112
303/792-9900

**American Humane
Education Society**
350 S. Huntington Avenue
Boston, MA 02130
617/522-7400

**American Society for the
Prevention of Cruelty to Animals**
441 E. 92nd Street
New York, NY 10128
212/876-7700

The Doris Day Animal League
900 2nd Street NE, Suite 303
Washington, DC 20002
202/842-3325

Friends of Animals, Inc.
P.O. Box 1244
Norwalk, CT 06856
203/866-5223

**The Humane Society of the
United States**
2100 L Street NW
Washington, DC 20037
202/452-1100

**National Humane
Education Society**
521A East Market Street
Leesburg, VA 22075
703/777-8319

**Pets Are Wonderful Council
(P.A.W.)**
500 N. Michigan Avenue,
Suite 200
Chicago, IL 60611
312/836-7145

Dog Registry and Activity Organizations

American Kennel Club
51 Madison Avenue
New York, NY 10010
212/696-8200

Delta Society (for Therapy Dogs)
P.O. Box 1080
Renton, WA 98057
206/226-7357

**Mixed Breed Dog Club
of America**
c/o Chris Dane
100 Acacia Avenue
San Bruno, CA 94066
415/588-1203

Project BREED
Network for Ani-Males and
Females
18707 Curry Powder Lane
Germantown, MD 20874-2014
301/428-3675

Therapy Dogs International
6 Hilltop Road
Mendham, NJ 07945
201/543-0888

United Kennel Club
Registration Department
100 East Kilgore Road
Kalamazoo, MI 49001
616/343-9020

United States Dog Agility
Association, Inc.
P.O. Box 850955
Richardson, TX 75085-0955
214/231-9700